CHURCH
IN A MARXIST SOCIETY

Jan Milič Lochman

CHURCH
IN A MARXIST SOCIETY
A CZECHOSLOVAK VIEW

HARPER & ROW, PUBLISHERS

NEW YORK, EVANSTON, AND LONDON

Portions of this book are based upon the author's earlier writings, the titles of which are as follows:
"Humanization in a Socialist Society," in *Christianity and Crisis,* May 13, 1968.
"Christianity and Marxism: Convergence and Divergence," in *Christianity and Crisis,* May 12, 1969.
"The Lordship of Christ in a Secularized World," in *Lutheran World,* 1967, No. 1.
"The Gospel for Atheists," in *Theology Today,* October 1969.
"The Service of the Church in a Socialist Society," in *Christian Social Ethics in a Changing World,* edited by John C. Bennett (New York: Association Press, 1966).

FIRST EDITION

LIBRARY OF CONGRESS CATALOG CARD NUMBER: 77-85067

To
President John C. Bennett
and the community of the
Union Theological Seminary
in New York City

CONTENTS

7

THEOLOGY IN DIALOGUE

PREFACE

A few years ago, I had the opportunity to discuss theology's changing situation in our contemporary world
with a leading West German theologian. He summed up
the changes from his point of view with a slogan: *the end
of the close-time for theologians.* During the fifties in
West Germany—as in some other Western countries—
theology still enjoyed a certain privileged status within
its cultural and academic establishment. The theologians
played an important role in practically all areas of public
life and they played it with unquestioned authority. In

the sixties, this role changed. It became much more controversial. The Church and its theology came under the attack of the younger "skeptical generation," as did all the other preestablished authorities. The traditional privileges were radically questioned. Within the intellectual community a climate of growing criticism surrounded theology. Thus indeed the end of the "close-time" for theologians was at hand.

In listening to this analysis of the place of theology in contemporary society and culture, I realized that in my own environment the changes were paradoxically different. I proposed another slogan as more appropriate to our Czechoslovak situation: *the end of the quarantine for theologians*. This was indeed a remarkable change. In the fifties, our churches were pretty much in a ghetto situation. We were cut off from ecumenical fellowship with Christian churches in other countries, especially in the early part of that decade. At that time we were also separated from the dominant trends in our society, particularly from contact with Marxist philosophers. We were aware then of the theological problem involved in such a quarantine, but we had accepted the mistrust of our socialist society as a judgment on the church's shortcomings with respect to the issues of social justice in the past. We remembered, however, that genuine repentance could not mean passivity. It necessarily involved patient self-critical effort to transcend this situation and to work toward more openness between our church and our society. This happened with remarkable intensity in the sixties.

This development had two aspects. The first was the possibility that emerged in the sixties for relationship with the *ecumenical community*. While Czech theology had been "ecumenical-minded" from its foundations in the Bohemian Reformation, it remained for a large part of the fifties a somewhat "Platonic vision"—an impossible dream. This changed in the sixties. In 1961 the first All-Christian Peace Assembly in Prague made this city one of the centers of ecumenical activity in the last decade. The ecumenical contacts developed so intensively and extensively that we, as minority churches and small theological faculties, were nearly overwhelmed and had occasionally to struggle for breath for our own work in church and society.

At the same time, our active cooperation within the World Council of Churches had been growing considerably since its General Assembly in New Delhi 1961. I personally was very fortunate to be asked to serve on the Working Committee on Church and Society, which proved to be of unique importance for the whole ecumenical movement. The continuing exchange between this group of dedicated theologians and social scientists was a stimulating experience. So too was my involvement with the World Conference on Church and Society in Geneva 1966 and the Uppsala Assembly 1968. These unforgettable confrontations of the worldwide church with the emerging worldwide society became an enduring challenge to my theological attempts.

Not less important was the second aspect, namely, the positive developments in our own *socialist society*. The quarantine of the fifties was challenged in the sixties, with the Christian-Marxist dialogue clearing the way. In the beginning it was not easy. Prejudices on both sides blocked mutual understanding. Nevertheless, the dialogue developed from very modest beginnings into a phenomenon of considerable spiritual importance. One of the most encouraging experiences in our existence as churches in a Marxist society was the new depth of our encounter with the Marxists—the discovery that we have a great deal to say to each other, in spite of all our ideological differences, and that we even might mean a great deal to one another.

At the same time, the practical cooperation between Christians and Marxists as citizens of a socialist society reached a new level. With unique intensity, this happened in the memorable year of 1968 as a result of the attempts at a far-reaching democratization of our socialist society. A "subject-object relation," so typical of the Stalinist era in which the citizens—particularly the citizens of a non-conformist creed—were often considered as an object of political administration, was challenged. New relations of growing mutual respect and solidarity developed in the common search for the humanization of our society. Thus Czechoslovak Christians started to play a new role in their cultural and social environment.

In this connection, one aspect might deserve widespread attention. The new opportunity and mission within our society was not found by a church selling out its "strange" Biblical vision and trying to adapt the Good News to the spirit of the times. On the contrary. The Czech theologian, in his movement toward greater participation in the public life of his country, was not expected to leave his theology in the cloakroom. He was not welcome only as another exponent of general common sense and general goodwill. In my encounters with the intellectual community of a predominantly Marxist orientation I found again and again that an attempt to bear witness to that "strange love" and "radical vision" of the Gospel was taken more seriously than any attempt to relativize or to water down the message into some general philanthropy and religion.

It is worthwhile noticing that in the time when some of the Western theologians started the God-is-dead talk, one of the creative Marxist thinkers in my country wrote his best-seller *God Is Not Quite Dead* (V. Gardavský). This is not just incidental. It might rather be indicative of the fact that a society committed to the program and political action of humanization needs a confrontation with that "ultimate concern" and radical vision entrusted to, and sometimes badly neglected by, theologians. Thus the way our theology came out of its cultural quarantine was not through relativizing but rather through strengthening our belief in the contribution which theology can make in secularized society today.

The following chapters are grounded in this basic conviction. They reflect some of the experiences and insights which I have gained in the years 1948–68 as a theologian of the Comenius Faculty in Prague, as a committed member of my Evangelical Church of Czech Brethren and an engaged citizen of my Czechoslovak society. Particularly, the chapters try to bear witness to those encouraging openings which we were able to find, in spite of all our losses, on our narrow yet hopeful way as churches in a radically secularized Marxist society.

The greater part of these chapters was shared with my students at the Union Theological Seminary in New York City in the academic year 1968–69—in fragments also with students at other American universities and seminaries. During that year I had the privilege of teaching—and learning—as the Harry Emerson Fosdick Visiting Professor of that great theological school. I shall always gratefully remember the atmosphere of intense intellectual exchange and imaginative Christian commitment as well as the warmth of the fellowship which I and my family found in the Seminary community. The dedication of this book to President John C. Bennett, my distinguished friend, symbolizes that gratitude.

Encouraged by the response I received from my stu-

dents and from other members of the "Union Family"—
some of whom, like Wesley Poorman, Richard Pachella,
and, particularly, Miss Babbie Mallery, helped considerably with technical preparations of the manuscript—I decided to present this book to the broader public. I am
aware of the risk involved in writing a book so firmly
rooted in a specific theological and social situation for
readers living in a rather different spiritual and cultural
context. If I venture this risk, I do so in the belief that in
our ecumenical world, a distinctive theological experience
need not remain a matter of indifference to Christians in
other places. My hope is that this account of the Czechoslovak experience might help us all to serve men in our
different churches and societies with new imagination,
humility, and courage.

July 1969   J.M.L.

CZECH
PROTESTANTISM:

ITS CONTEXT IN SPACE AND TIME

THE ECUMENICAL SIGNIFICANCE
OF EASTERN EUROPE

"I do not know who invited this gentleman into the United States. But it is clear that he is a Communist agent. There are no Christian theologians in Eastern Europe." These words were the first comment on a public lecture of mine in the United States in the fall of 1968. The speaker did not argue about what I tried to say in interpreting Christian life in a Marxist society. Rather he immediately questioned my "historical existence" and that of my friends—at least in the sense we try to live it: the existence of a Christian in a Marxist society. In its rudeness, this voice was certainly exceptional. In its way of argument, however, it was symptomatic of a certain distorted image of the religious situation in Eastern Europe.

This image was created and effectively publicized by Cold War propaganda. For many, it survives as an unquestioned stereotype even today. Eastern Europe (the Soviet Union, Bulgaria, Romania, Yugoslavia, Albania, Hungary, Poland, the German Democratic Republic, Czechoslovakia) is a "Communist-dominated area." The Communists have been known for their ideological opposition to religion and, on some occasions, for the policies of administrative pressures put against the churches. This experience is now absolutized and even mythologized: the "Communist world" is the area of the Antichrist. There is no place for Christian churches in such an area —at least not in an organized form. An "underground church" of anonymous martyrs driven into the catacombs remains the only Christian possibility. Any church representative emerging publicly from the Eastern European churches is dismissed with suspicion. Aren't they actually Communist agents? "There are no Christian theologians in Eastern Europe. . . ."

As long as this image of the religious situation in Eastern Europe is taken for granted, the idea that Eastern Europe can be significant for Christians in other parts of the world seems to be somehow unreal and even nonsensical. What is nonexistent cannot have true significance. The argument of this book is that this image is a distortion. Its thesis is that the experience of Christian churches in Eastern Europe is indeed ecumenically significant. It is a modest yet distinctive experience. Let me develop this thesis in a few words.

We speak of a *modest* experience: Eastern Europe is an area of deeply shattered Christian institutions. The propaganda image just mentioned is, of course, a distortion. Yet it deals with certain phenomena which cannot be denied. The "Communist world" is a region of programmatic alienation of official society from Christian churches. The degree of that alienation may differ in different countries, as may the ideological and administrative measures of state policies and the whole cultural climate surrounding the churches. Basically, however, the socialist societies of Eastern Europe understand themselves as "post-Christian." The churches ceased to be part and parcel of the cultural and social establishment. They all became, sometimes painfully, disestablished. Their members are Christians without privileges. It is with respect to these changes in the social and cultural status of Christian churches in Eastern Europe that I speak of a *modest* possibility which these churches ecumenically represent. It is modest especially as far as the social and cultural impact on their societies is concerned.

At the same time, however, the churches of Eastern Europe represent a *distinctive* ecumenical experience and contribution. They are by no means the only ones characterized by the modesty of their social and cultural possibilities. Many churches in other parts of the world face a similar situation in this respect. I think especially of the "younger churches" in Asia and Africa. These vigorous churches, whose challenging contribution is very much felt in the ecumenical movement today, are very often small minorities in their nations (especially in Asia). They are not repressed. On the contrary, sometimes they enjoy certain privileges. Yet traditionally they have been, and have remained, on the margin of their societies and cultures.

In this respect the situation in Eastern Europe is different. Traditionally, these are "Christian countries."

They can trace an old and distinguished heritage, both spiritually and culturally. They are not the oldest Christian churches—not to be compared with the churches of the Middle East in this respect. In their majority, though, they can look back to a history of more than one thousand years. In these centuries, important spiritual and ecclesiastical developments occurred in this area. Rich religious impulses and traditions have been displayed and a genuine "spiritual wealth" has been accumulated. It is worthwhile to note that this applies to all three major ecumenical spiritual families, all of which effectively shaped the religious face of Eastern Europe: Eastern Orthodoxy, Roman Catholicism, and Protestantism.

It has been, first of all, the *Eastern Orthodox* churches which have played an important role, especially in the east of Eastern Europe. The wealth of their distinctive spirituality and culture has been very much present there. The unique richness of liturgy and of the sacramental life with particular emphasis on the resurrected Christ; the depth of the personal devotion of its participant members, so moving to anybody attending Orthodox worship in Eastern Europe; the influence of the religious spirit in the arts (the icons and the architecture of the sanctuaries) as well as in literature (Dostoevski)—all these are examples of the presence of Orthodoxy in Eastern Europe.

This applies especially to the strongest of the Eastern churches, the Russian Orthodox Church. In its history, this church has been one of the most distinctive bodies of Christian spirituality. Even today it is one of the most important branches of ecumenical Christianity (a community of an estimated 50 million members). When the Russian Orthodox Church was accepted as a member church of the World Council of Churches in New Delhi in 1961, a new world (a very ancient world) of ecumenical experience was added to the ecumenical movement. In a similar way, other Eastern Orthodox churches have played a similar role within their own nations and cultures: the ancient Bulgarian Orthodox Church (6 million), the influential Romanian Orthodox Church (15 million), the Serbian Orthodox Church (7 million), and other smaller Orthodox churches in Eastern Europe. This polyphony of Eastern Orthodoxy is the first proof of the ecumenical significance of Eastern Europe.

The presence of the Orthodox heritage, however, does not exhaust the full richness of Christian tradition in Eastern Europe. There is also a very strong *Roman Catholic* presence in this part of the world. The clearest example of this is the Polish Catholic Church, which has been one of the strongest branches of European Catholicism (28 million), with great and sometimes dominant cultural and even political influence within its nation. Among Eastern European churches, this church probably tried hardest to preserve and enlarge its traditional privileges, even power-political positions, within the radically changed socialist society. Sometimes it did so more from the presuppositions of its mighty past than in genuinely searching for new ways and attitudes of the Christian church in a secularized society. Its considerable power and influence, however, cannot be doubted.

There are other East European countries with strong Roman Catholic churches, such as Hungary (a country of a strong Catholic majority of an estimated 6 million), Yugoslavia (6 million, especially in its Croatian part), and, of course, also Czechoslovakia (about 7 million), even though Catholicism in this rather secularized country cannot be compared in vigor and influence to that of Poland. If we add to these Catholic churches a certain renaissance of the Uniate groups (Christians who are of

Eastern rite but recognize Roman authority), especially in Czechoslovakia since 1968, the presence of the Roman Catholic heritage in Eastern Europe becomes clearly visible.

What is the situation of the *Protestant* churches in this area? Division of Europe into the East and the West is in some respects and in some places arbitrary—as in the division of Germany. Yet for our purpose in the concrete situation of Europe today it is characteristic that some of the strongest provinces of traditional German Protestantism (estimated 14 million) belong to the German Democratic Republic. The "motherland" of the Reformation has become a part of a socialist country. The celebrations of the Reformation anniversary in 1967 in Wittenberg underlined this fact. Thus the historical strongholds of German Protestantism lie in Eastern Europe—for example, the Evangelical Church of Berlin Brandenburg, the Lutheran churches of Saxony, Mecklenburg, and Thüringen.

These are strong majority churches in their respective regions. But there are also active Protestant minority churches in Eastern Europe. There is, first of all, the Hungarian Protestantism of both the Reformed (2 million) and the Lutheran (430,000) type. There are Protestant churches in Romania (1 million, also among the German- and Hungarian-speaking citizens). There are strong Protestant movements in the Soviet Union, especially dynamic groups of Baptists (estimated 2 million) and Lutherans (about 2 million) in the Baltic republics. And there is, of course, Czechoslovak Protestantism (1.5 million), both in the Czech part of the country and in Slovakia. Thus this third branch of ecumenical Christianity today is well represented in Eastern Europe also.

Our short survey about the Christianity in Eastern Europe anticipates what will be dealt with in more detail in the following chapters, namely, the thesis that Christian churches in Eastern Europe represent an important branch of Christianity historically—and today. The dialectics of its difficult social and cultural situation in a radically secularized and alienated environment, and the richness and multiformity of its historical resources, make for its ecumenical distinctiveness and significance. Christian existence in Eastern Europe is a meaningful theme for ecumenical study and consideration.

This theme might be valid particularly with respect to the churches in the West—in Western Europe and also in the United States. These churches share with East European churches the richness and multiformity of their spiritual traditions. Their social and cultural condition is very different—at least at first glance—for churches in the West do not live under an organized challenge of a powerful ideology and its educational thrust. On the contrary, generally they are still part and parcel of their social and cultural establishment. And yet if we analyze more carefully the signs and the streams of the times, the established position of churches in the West within their respective culture and society is no longer unchallenged. The progressive secularization in modern technologically advanced societies alienated vast segments of the population from organized churches and their religion. And the radical social movements—such as the emerging black movements in the United States—question with much moral strength the traditional and privileged positions of churches within the established systems. Thus the strong Western churches stand also on the threshold —or better, in the midst—of a serious cultural and social crisis.

In facing the crisis, the experience of Eastern European Christians might be of some unexpected actuality for the West. They have gone through situations and have gathered experiences which—*mutatis mutandis*—might become situations and experiences of the future of churches in the West, certainly not in the same way (probably without that element of an open and "official" ideological opposition), yet with a similar challenge. Thus the yesterday and today of Christian existence in Eastern Europe might become the tomorrow and today of Christian existence in the West. Therefore, it seems worthwhile—especially in this age of close ecumenical contact and cooperation—to give deeper attention to the life and reflections of East European Christianity. With some ecumenical imagination, it might help Christians in other situations to draw some lessons from both its crisis and its struggles, and from its new discoveries and chances, especially in seeking and finding new ways for a more credible Christian existence in a radically secularized society.

This book tries to present a very modest contribution to such an ecumenical exchange and search. It thinks and speaks from one particular aspect of East European experience: that of a Czechoslovak Christian, particularly a Czech Protestant. As such it can in no way pretend to put forward and interpret the whole range of Christian existence in Eastern Europe. The Czechoslovak experience is specific and relatively narrow. Czech Protestantism is a minority church, in many respects much weaker than some other churches of Eastern Europe. All Protestant denominations in Czechoslovakia have about 1.5 million members out of the predominantly Catholic population of 14 million. Thus a voice of a Czechoslovak

Protestant cannot lay any claim to representative character.

On the other hand, this modest branch of East European Christianity has some specific significance for our theme. It has played a certain pioneering role in its reflections on the tasks and mission of the Christian church in a socialist society, both in facing the representatives of its own environment and in interpreting this experience on the ecumenical scene. This is, of course, in no way some special merit of this Protestantism or a proof of its superiority. Rather, some specific conditions encouraged concentrated endeavor in this respect. Let us mention at least three of them.

Preexisting *geographical* and cultural reasons urged Czechoslovak Protestants toward ecumenical reflection and exchange. Czechoslovakia is situated on the crossroads of the European East and West. It is a socialist country with a traditionally prevalent (not exclusively) Western cultural orientation. In this position, it has been forced again and again to ask the question of the meaning of its history, to reflect on its mission, and to seek a dialogue with people in other places and situations.

Confessional reasons further explain why it was Czech Protestantism—though it was weaker than, for example, the Catholic Church in its neighborhood—which concentrated on this task. To reflect on the social and historical responsibility of the Christian church is, of course, by no means an exclusive prerogative of Protestantism. It is a matter of concern to all Christians. Yet this task is imposed on Protestant groups with greater urgency—not because they are more "enlightened," but simply because reflection is the very element of Protestant faith. For an Eastern Orthodox Church the emphasis is different: its classical heritage and uncomparable witness is more concerned with the "sacramental presence" of the church in the world, the permeation of individual and social life by the spirit of Christian devotion and love. Orthodox churches have displayed this spirit with great fidelity. Compared with this emphasis, the witness of intellectual reflection and dialogue with people of different traditions has been considered relatively unimportant, whereas for Protestants it is a primary task. If they give it up or if they underestimate it—for example, if they become fundamentalists without concern for the new interpretation of their faith in a changed situation—they miss a substantial part of their own heritage. The church of the Word has to be concerned about the interpretation of its vision in dialogue.

There are, finally, strong *historical* and spiritual reasons for this orientation of Czech Protestantism. In its historical background there were strong motives enabling a positive understanding of a radically changed socialist society. We shall deal with these theological accents of the Czech reformation in a special chapter. Here it is worth mentioning that the strong emphasis on the biblical vision of the Kingdom of God in its specific orientation toward the needs of the underprivileged, as well as its conception of the church as a "community of pilgrims," a "church without privileges," encouraged Czechoslovak Protestants to seek a positive orientation within a socialist society changed by revolution. The theme of a radical social change was not imposed on these Christians simply from the outside (as was the case with the majority of churches in other parts of Eastern Europe). Thus they did not painfully have to seek for categories for dealing with the new situation. For example, the category of the "judgment of God," so important for Hungarian churches and their theology in the effort to cope theologically with socialist revolution, was never the only key to our under-standing of a church's place or task within a socialist so-ciety. There was a broad positive encouragement to get involved, to interpret, to act.

Nobody could claim that these talents and potential-ities were really displayed with corresponding creativity and boldness in the actual practice of Czechoslovak Prot-estants. Much confusion, inertia, and lack of courage existed among them. There were also serious difficulties and obstacles from the outside, as we shall see. Yet there are some indications that the talents were not completely buried or lost. In a modest way, Czechoslovak churches were indeed able to act in a pioneering way. Let me sug-gest at least two such examples.

1. *Christian Peace Conference.* In 1958, a group of forty Christians from different (mostly East-European) countries came together in Prague for a "Christian Peace Conference." There was much distrust concerning this conference—both in the ecumenical public abroad and in the churches at home. Was this organization something more than the instrument of East European political propaganda? The Christian Peace Conference undoubt-edly had to struggle with such temptations, including the problem of its own one-sidedness. Yet the movement proved to have a sound core and a passion for reconcilia-tion and peaceful coexistence which proved quite capable of correcting ecumenical one-sidedness. In its first decade, it grew into an important international Christian body. The three All-Christian Peace Assemblies—all held in Prague —in 1961, 1964, and 1968 gathered together a broad representation of Christians from all parts of the world. The conference clearly focused on questions of peace. Yet at the same time it has become an important ecumenical experiment. Its role as a channel for ecumenical contacts

and cooperation, especially for Christians from Eastern Europe, has been of great value. This conference was the first meeting place for most Christians from Eastern Europe and, as such, was the starting point in their ecumenical exchange and cooperation. Much new theological searching in Eastern Europe has been developed in connection with this movement.

All this activity originated and has been organized on the initiative of Czechoslovak Protestantism, whose pioneering role within the East European ecumenical context is illustrated in this way.

2. *Openings for a dialogue.* We mentioned already that Czechoslovak Protestants played a specific role in interpreting a Christian existence in a socialist society, both to their fellow Christians abroad and to their ideological partners in their own society. This effort was connected especially with the thought and work of the leading Czech theologian of the last generation: Josef L. Hromádka. Hromádka, who spent part of his life during World War II as a highly inspiring teacher at Princeton Theological Seminary, is one of the few prophetic theologians and churchmen, not only in Eastern Europe but in the ecumenical movement in general. He proved to be such a pioneering theologian and leader especially, and repeatedly, within the Czechoslovak context. Even prior to World War II he was one of the first who tried to prepare his church to face the crisis of European liberalism—which for Czechoslovakia had its tragic culmination in the capitulation of Western democracies in their confrontation with Hitler at Munich in 1938—in a search for a deeper theological orientation. He was one of the first who tried to open a positive perspective in the encounter with the socialist revolution of 1948. And he was again among the first to endorse creative attempts at the

democratization of the socialist society and to protest against the interruption of that process in August, 1968.

Hromádka was exceptionally qualified to open an East European dialogue both with the ecumenical movement and with the Marxists in his own society. He was often criticized and even rejected—in the ecumenical movement and in his own church. Some of his decisions and actions (or omissions) were indeed controversial. Yet he was an incomparable witness to, and interpreter of, a creative Christian orientation in a socialist society. In this capacity he emerged as one of the leaders of the ecumenical movement in Amsterdam in 1948—where he was a strong opponent of John Foster Dulles and his anti-Communist picture of the world situation—in Evanston in 1954, and again in New Delhi in 1961.

Hromádka did not remain alone in his effort for ecumenical dialogue. He assembled around himself a whole group of younger theologians and churchmen (particularly in his own Comenius Faculty of Theology in Prague), who tried to carry on his theological and ecumenical work. The active and effective participation of Czechoslovak Christians in ecumenical thought and action (especially during the World Conference on Church and Society in Geneva in 1966 and in Uppsala in 1968) is a vivid illustration of some success of this endeavor. The ecumenical contribution of Czechoslovak Protestantism is evidently stronger than its minority character would suggest.

Still more important than this ecumenical activity have become the pioneering attempts at opening dialogue within our own socialist society. This was a rather delicate and difficult task. For the official ideology of the fifties, Christian experience, considered simply as "the opiate of the people," was basically meaningless, even dangerous. Consequently, there was no strong interest in communication. Practical arrangements were necessary as long as the churches existed. But this interim period was considered more or less as an emergency, eventually to be solved—religion would disappear. Thus, there was no real readiness for interpretation and dialogue. Only two modalities were considered functional: a militant atheist propaganda or ideological silence around the churches and their world of religion.

To some church groups of a more fundamentalist orientation this situation, though certainly not the ideal one, seemed somehow acceptable. Not so to theologically more alert groups of theologians and laymen. A patient search for a genuine encounter started—for an encounter not in a "subject-object" attitude but rather in an "existential interpretation," an authentic dialogue. The opening of that dialogue constituted a major achievement and change in the last years. The concluding chapter of this book is devoted to these developments. Here we only list this process as a phenomenon of great importance. The Christians were consciously and openly recognized not only as citizens but as citizens of their specific faith and creed; not as objects of cultural policy and ideological "care" but as socialist partners of another creed, as fully "normal" citizens in their society. Active and creative participation in the life of society included intellectual and spiritual spheres. This brought a change to the possibilities for Christian existence in Eastern Europe. Together with other Christians, and in cooperation with their Marxist partners, Czech Protestants tried to contribute in opening new perspectives for the church in a socialist society.

THE HISTORICAL HERITAGE
OF CZECH PROTESTANTISM

THE CZECH PROTESTANT MOVEMENT   Czech
Protestantism has an especially lengthy and tragic history.
The Reformation in Bohemia and Moravia really began
a century earlier than it did in the other European countries. A reform movement started at the beginning of the
fifteenth century after the beginnings of reform in the
fourteenth century with Konrad von Waldhausen, Jan
Milič of Kroměříž, and Mathias of Janov. It is associated with the name of Jan Hus (1372–1415). An outstanding scholar, theologian, and preacher, Hus possibly

had not yet acquired the consistent clarity of Reformation thought known to Martin Luther and John Calvin. However, in principle, Hus broke through boundaries of the medieval system and basically moved toward the Reformation with his decisive claim of Scripture as the sovereign source of authority in all ecclesiastical tradition. This applied not only to theory but (with special radicality) to concrete grievances, both in the church's institutional and in its social life.

The Magna Charta of the Hussite movement, the Four Articles of Prague, in which the Hussite program is set forth in succint formulations, shows this convincingly. These four articles set forth the following points: (1) the Word of God is to be preached freely; (2) the holy sacrament of the Last Supper is to be served in form of both bread and wine (*sub utraque*); (3) priest and monk are to relinquish earthly position and possession, and all are to begin an obedient life based on the apostolic model of poverty; (4) all mortal sins are to be punished, and public sinners in that condition are to be restrained. In these formulations are already emphasized what were later called the *notae verae ecclesiae,* the marks of the true church as the Lutheran Church, and especially the Reformed Church, understood them: the Word of God, the biblically grounded sacrament, and the discipline of the obedient life.

After Jan Hus' death as a martyr at Constance in 1415, the Hussite movement expanded into all of Bohemia and Moravia as a decidedly popular movement. Almost the entire population became Hussite, including many Germans. (Hus himself said that in his opinion "a good German is more precious than a bad brother.") Indeed, several men from other countries joined the movement. At its beginnings, the Hussite movement was very dynamic both spiritually (the Hussites were well versed in biblical knowledge) and socially. But certainly after years of warlike and spiritual wrestling with powers of the counterreformation (and its crusaders, whom the Hussites effectively defied), Hussitism weakened inside and out. The Hussites turned to so-called Utraquism, a reformed church created with a strongly conservative character, but still one in which a serious impulse toward biblical Christianity was never abandoned.

The true evangelical inspirations nevertheless were represented especially by the *Unitas Fratrum* (the Unity of Brethren) which arose about 1457 out of a handful of determined Christians. They gathered in the small town of Kunvald in east Bohemia in order to build there a real Christian community, one fashioned after the apostolic model. The *Unitas Fratrum* expanded in Bohemia and Moravia, but it always remained a small minority in the population. Furthermore, throughout almost all its history it was persecuted or suffered great duress. Nevertheless, the Unity of Brethren presented, in its profound spiritual resources as well as through its particular cultural achievements, the clearest phenomenon of Czech religious life in the sixteenth and seventeenth centuries. Here one thinks of its eminent theologians and thinkers, such as Lukas of Prague, Jan Blahoslav, and especially Jan Amos Comenius (1592–1670).

This promising development of Czech Protestantism applied not only to the Unity of Brethren but also to the Utraquist Church (to which 90 percent of the people belonged). Considerably enriched by its contact with the German and Swiss reformations, it became more evangelical. However, this promising development was tragically destroyed in 1620. The Protestant army and its king, Friedrich von der Pfalz, were defeated in the Battle of the White Mountain, near Prague, by the fanatically Catholic Hapsburgs. A ruthless counterreformation, certainly one of the most thorough in all Europe, was waged in Bohemia and Moravia. The leaders of the evangelical aristocracy were put to death, the evangelical faith was labeled a crime against the state, free citizens were driven either to become Catholic or to flee, and the subjects bound to the soil were simply impressed into the Catholic religion without any choice. Protestant life in Bohemia and Moravia was crippled during the long decades of the counterreformation. For many good reasons, this time was called "the era of darkness."

Finally, after 150 years (in 1781), the Edict of Toleration was issued by Austrian Emperor Joseph II, who realized the political and spiritual dangers both of oppression and of open resistance from the underground evangelical groups, especially in Moravia. This edict assured the remainder of the evangelical churches a limited toleration. In spite of the radical operations of the counterreformation, more than 70,000 of the "quiet ones in the land" now opted for the evangelical faith. They wanted to hold on to the legacy of the Czech reformation bequeathed by the Hussites and the Brethren. But that was not permitted, as they could choose only to become Lutheran or Reformed. Thus there grew up in our country a Lutheran Church and a Reformed Church. Both met hard times. During the Catholic rule of the Hapsburgs, both were merely tolerated and for decades not given equal rights. As late as 1861 and, in a real sense, only after the fall of the Hapsburg Monarchy in 1918 did they secure equal rights. In 1918 the old wish was finally granted, as both Czech evangelical churches united on a basis of the Czech reformation. They were now called the Evangelical Church of the Czech Brethren. A new era of Czech Protestantism had begun.

The "First Republic," under Thomas G. Masaryk, created favorable conditions for its positive development. Union with Slovakia (where, owing to a less strict counterreformation, the percentage of the Protestants was higher) strengthened the Protestant position in the nation. The Protestant churches grew considerably. Many people joined them from nationalistic motives, protesting the age-long alliance between Hapsburgs and the Roman Catholic Church. A whole new church, the Czechoslovak Church, arose out of such an away-from-Rome movement. But exactly the presence of the national element and sometimes of superficial anti-Catholicism made new theological reflection and orientation necessary. Under the spiritual leadership of the new Jan Hus Theological Faculty (the predecessor of the Comenius Faculty), this orientation was found in new emphases on biblical theology (Fr. Žilka and especially Sl. Daněk), in new appreciation of the "classical line of Christianity" (J. L. Hromádka), and in new interpretations of the heritage of the Czech reformation. This orientation helped the churches to overcome the collapse of the liberal democracy of 1938. The war with its dangers and German oppression brought a serious outward crisis. Some of the most active church members died in concentration camps. At the same time, a spiritual and theological deepening grew through the difficult years. A new generation of theologians (under the very able leadership of Josef B. Souček) was rising within the church, and also a new generation of biblically oriented laymen. Thus, the church was not entirely unprepared to meet a new challenge: the challenge of the emerging socialist society.

THEOLOGICAL ACCENTS OF THE CZECH REFORMATION   I have not presented this short historical survey merely for the sake of general information. Our historical orientation can have a deeper meaning: our actual situation as churches, our theological existence today, can scarcely be understood without that historical background. Naturally that is true for any church. It lives and moves in the "community of pilgrims," not only in space, in the ecumenical community of its contemporaries, but also in time, in the community of faith with its forefathers and brethren. The Christian always lives from the heritage of his ancestors. But there are definite times and situations in which this general relationship means much more than a historical background; rather, it is a supporting basis, a sustaining ground for critical orientation and inspiration. In this sense we in our congregations, embedded in the revolutionary movements of our time, have actively experienced this strengthening and binding presence of our church history. I want to illustrate in the following five points the relevance of this supporting background of the Czech reformation for our theological and ecclesiastical existence today.

1. The fundamental emphasis of the Bohemian reformation is, to start with, the concept of *evangelical obedience*. To believe means to be obedient, to live in the discipleship of Jesus Christ. Perhaps this was a characteristic gift of the Czech reformation. It realized in a serious and practical way that it is not enough just to teach (even though the significance of pure doctrine was never underrated, for doctrine is also a form of obedient existence). It is more important to live obediently, not only to *know* the truth but to *do* the truth. Jan Hus saw and lived that. To him, truth was not only insight into the structure of being (as Greek *aletheia*) but also the supporting, challenging, binding reality of the living God himself (as Hebrew *emeth*). That is why faith is obedience. And to be obedient means to shape all decisions

within the light of the basic conviction that "the truth of the Lord will prevail."

The "objective" presupposition of this understanding of faith is the emphasis on the royal authority of Jesus Christ. Of course the Hussites and the Brethren knew that Jesus Christ is our only *Priest* (to express it in the conceptuality of the traditional Reformation doctrine of the "three offices" of Jesus Christ). He is Priest and Savior and Redeemer of the world. He is the Lamb who bears the sins of the world, the Mediator who reconciles us to God. Of course they also knew that he is our unsurpassable *Prophet,* the final revealer of God and man, himself *the* Truth. But, they also asserted, he is our sovereign *King.* Perhaps this is their special emphasis. He is the Lord, the only Lord of the church and the only Lord of the world. His Kingdom comes. The eschatological expectation of the Bohemian reformation is enormously active. It is necessary to live in the light of this coming Kingdom and to shape the passing world in conformity to it. This is true with respect to the church *and* to society. Certainly we do not establish the Kingdom of God by our endeavors. Except for the radical groups at the beginnings of the movement, the Hussites and the Brethren were not "enthusiasts" (*Schwärmer*). But the Kingdom presses in upon us and obligates us, and it intends to change our life.

In this understanding, the Kingdom of God challenged the structures of the given order, specifically the worldly power of the "Constantinian Church" and the social injustice of the established "Christian society." The Hussites recognized in the Bible an entirely different image of social justice than that imbodied in the traditional social order. They also knew that one must obey the Word of God more than any ecclesiastical tradition.

Therefore it is urgent to transform the worldly order. That is the significance of the ventures both of the Hussites, from their beginnings up to the attempts at apostolic communism in the city of Tabor, and of the Brethren in their striving to take seriously the Word of Jesus as the authoritative rule in a literal sense as they applied it to the practical sphere of personal and civil life. In these ventures we may uncover traces of "enthusiasm" (*Schwärmerei*). The "second reformation" (I am referring especially to the Lutheran and Reformed movements) is in many respects perhaps more sober and doctrinally purer. On the other hand, we should ask whether in that Reformation something rather decisive was not lost in its "pure doctrine." (Here I am referring, for example, to the nearly dualistic separation of the "two kingdoms" of Lutheran orthodoxy with its temptation to suspend the normative significance of the Word of God for the formation of the secular sphere.) We may ask whether the "first reformation" was not really essentially right in its insistence that the formal principles of the classic Reformation (*sola scriptura*) should be applied not only to matters of doctrine and church but to all the strata of life in church and society. This should be done not in an enthusiastic-legalistic imitation of biblical commandments but in the spirit of obedient discipleship. But it should be done. Then faith is obedience.

2. A predominant part of the history of the Czech church is its history as a *church of the martyrs*. I understand this concept not merely as a characterization of the *ecclesia pressa*, suffering church. One could certainly apply that designation to the history of the evangelical church in Bohemia and Moravia. Perhaps we could say with much justification that they suffered more than many other European churches. They had their martyrs, begin-

ning with Jan Hus. When Comenius wrote his short history of the Czech church, he could justifiably call it *The History of the Harsh Afflictions of the Czech Church.* In a certain sense our church has always been a suffering church, the community beneath the cross, not a church of visible triumph and splendor. But never was martyrdom celebrated as an end in itself.

If we subsequently use the term "church of martyrs," our interest is in its broader sense, as that term is understood in the New Testament. *Marturia* is a testimony, a confession, above all something very concrete: a testimony of the cross, a confession of Jesus Christ the crucified. Indeed, this testimony was clearly uttered in the Czech reformation. Certainly the church lives in faith in the Resurrected One, and so it is already in the light of the resurrection. The Czech reformation never fostered an isolated "cross" or "suffering" theology. But it knew very clearly that on this earth the way of the disciple is the way beneath the cross. This is true even if its discipleship is rooted in the power of the resurrection and practiced in the hope of the coming Lord. We stand under the cross until the end of the world, and we are obligated to remain there. This means that the church of Jesus is not summoned to rule over this world. Here we have in mind the Prague Articles and their call to apostolic poverty. The church is called to serve. Its goal is not first to assert its own prestige and privileges, but to fulfill its mission. This mission is given it by God, and so it is in no way bound to the favor or disfavor of the world.

The churches of the Czech reformation (especially the Czech Brethren) understood themselves in that way, not as a self-centered institution but as an eccentric community. That means a community whose center is not borne in itself. It is a *communio viatorum* (community on the way), a band of pilgrims who have not yet reached their goal and who are still on the way. It is a society of debtors who know very soberly with the Apostle Paul that they are in debt to "the Greeks and barbarians, the wise and the foolish," even to the pious and atheist. Thus the church does not understand itself as "master of creation" but as servant, as a church of the martyrs in the comprehensive sense of that word. All these conceptions, "community of pilgrims," "society of debtors," "society of service," and naturally the self-understanding of the church expressed by these images, have proved their orienting and supporting power clearly in past decades of our church. These concepts help us to seek and find our place as the church in a world of significant social changes, the place on which, in all the variations of history, we can stand and act. It is the place of service, the place of witness.

3. The churches of the Czech reformation were always *churches of the people*. They arose from a free national movement and, throughout almost all their history, were tied to the common people. This is true except for the conservative period of the Utraquist Church. Perhaps there is a difference here in comparison with the German (and other European) established churches (*Landeskirchen*). It is true that the German reformation was also a national movement. Nevertheless the German reformation churches were organized "from above downward," under the patronage of the provincial rulers. That may have been a historic necessity, but it was also a serious danger and drawback. In this way the official churches became too one-sidedly related to the ruling powers of their nation. The intimate association of throne and altar with the ruling figure as the *summus episcopus* (chief

bishop) and the church as the support for the established ruling powers was taken for granted. Alienation of the larger segment of working people was the fatal consequence.

It was otherwise, however, with Czech protestantism. In our country the reformation was instituted not from above but from below. Even during the era of the victories of the reformation in our country, that reformation never became a matter for the politically and socially privileged; precisely the opposite, it was always a broad-based movement of the population. Especially in the first period of the movement, the victory of the Hussite was the victory of the revolution over economic and spiritual oppression. It was the way out from under political and spiritual bondage. And even after its defeat the reformation remained, during the long centuries of persecution and oppression, still linked closely to the underprivileged people. Only the poorest of the poor remained faithful; only those who did not strive and hope for a civic career formed the community of the churches in the era of toleration. Certainly this situation has been altered at last. Especially since the end of the nineteenth century, Czech Protestantism has developed as a preponderantly middle-class church. Nevertheless, the tradition of close relationships with the lower social classes has persisted. Up until today the Czech Evangelical Church has understood itself to be a church of the people.

It is clear how helpful this element of the historical heritage of the Bohemian reformation can be for an unprejudiced orientation of the church in a socialist society.

4. The Czech reformation was always *ecumenically oriented*. All-Christian unity and, in particular, the unity of the reformation were always supported. The first steps of the Czech reformation seem, however, to contradict

this claim. The Bohemian reformation, and especially the Unity of Brethren, was really the first movement in Western Christianity successfully to assert and constitute itself an independent church against the Church of Rome. It has never regretted this step. The oneness of the church is in no way considered to be an absolute value. There can be no genuine unity if that unity comes at the cost of the freedom and truth of the Word of God. In that case, that such unity be challenged is not only permitted but mandatory. The Brethren broke from it on the basis of "the need for salvation," as they said repeatedly. But they have never given up the acknowledgment and vision of a deep inclusive unity of all Christians.

This is already evident in the name the Brethren chose for themselves. The Brethren refused to call themselves the church. In their view there is only one single church, the body of Jesus Christ, who can have his faithful members in different church communities. And it follows directly from this that no earthly community can call itself the church without further explanation. That is why the Brethren speak rather of different "unities," even the "Roman unity." They do this to reserve the precious name of "church" for the body of Christ. For the Christian, consequently, there is the need to preserve an open horizon toward the other "unities," to take up an unprejudiced hopeful search for brethren and also to include the unexpected and perhaps unfamiliar brother in this category. The Brethren actually did this in an exemplary way. As soon as they learned of a group of truly Christian persuasion anywhere, they took the trouble to get in touch with them. This applied to Luther and, later, to the theologians of the Swiss reformation. The Brethren also turned eastward, to their Orthodox brothers. They traveled and had conversations with them.

This consciousness of all-Christian and especially all-Protestant unity was developed and deepened by Comenius. We can rightly describe him as the *homo oecumenicus* (ecumenical man) of his era. He suffered from the hardening of the interconfessional lines inside the Protestantism of his day, and he did his best to bridge its lamentable divisions. His *Testament of the Dying Mother-Unity of Czech Brethren* and other writings show his profound conviction in the fundamental unity of the Reformation as well as his passionate endeavors to take practical steps to realize this unity in reciprocal relationships among Christian communities. So for us, in the present day, the legacy of the Czech reformation has been a living inspiration toward ecumenical cooperation.

5. The movement of Czech Protestantism always emphasized the *peace mission* of Christian communities. It was, strictly speaking, not a pacifist movement. Not even the Unity of Brethren can be counted among the historic peace churches, such as the Mennonites and Quakers. The pacifism of principle remained only a small, even if theologically and spiritually influential, minority. But the concern for peace itself and the church's task of fostering peace belong to the basic emphases of the theological and practical work of the Czech reformation. It existed from the initial impulse of the Hussite movement. This assertion may appear to be extravagant. If one thinks back to the Hussite beginnings, there is by no means only peace and gentleness—precisely the opposite. There were bloody demonstrations and disturbances, even year-long wars. This was a war of resistance, of defense against the aggression of the counterreformation that swept Europe. It was, in the traditional sense, a *bellum justum* (just war), but nevertheless it was war.

However, it was not war, but peace, that was closest

to Hussite hearts. In the midst of the battles, again and again were heard the calls for peace. And not merely that, but a sharp self-criticism also existed in relation to the matter of violence, even "legitimate violence." One distinguished advocate of this criticism was Petr Chelčický, a sharp-minded thinker who arose from the radical wing of the Hussite reform movement. His emphasis on the royal authority of Jesus Christ and on obedient discipleship to Jesus Christ linked him with the Hussites. Yet for him, Jesus remains the Prince of Peace, the Lord of nonviolence. Jesus' power, measured in earthly terms, is nonviolent. Not war, but only peace, is allowed to be conjoined with his name. From this standpoint Chelčický raised a radical criticism not only against the society and church at hand but also against the Hussite movement itself. He became the conscience of the Hussite revolution.

At the end of this way, and in a sense like a peak, stands the figure of Jan Amos Comenius, the true *angelus pacis* (angel of peace) of his turbulent times. This theologian and teacher strenuously devoted himself to the indefatigable cause of peace. It is evident that he did this on the basis of the gospel, but he also worked it out very concretely in his constant endeavor to propose and take visible measures on the confused political and ecclesiastical stage. One need only read his *Panorthosia* to see how much of present-day conversations and proposals for peace were earlier put forth by him. He drafted plans for an international board of directors of worldly governments, an international peace court, and a plan for general disarmament. The spirit of violence, he maintained, should be opposed not just in the final course of things when there is an armed "hot war" but at its very beginnings as well, in concern for stopping the mistrust that is generated between the peoples of the world and in the clash of ideologies (what we today call Cold War). This was very urgent in his time, the era of worsening relations and a growing spirit of oppression between the churches, even within Protestantism. How strenuously Comenius battled against this demonic spirit! And how thoroughly had he reflected and planned! His ecumenical plans were tightly bound to his suggestions for peace. He planned a world consistory, a worldwide church assembly which was conceived as the international connecting link between the churches. He proposed an ecumenical council which would not only oversee inner Christian business (a universal reformation) but also alleviate the general miseries of mankind by establishing a way of "light, peace, and salvation." The plans for the ecumenical church and the plans for peace belong inseparably together because they are really to be understood as acts of obedient faith in the discipleship of Jesus Christ.

In continuity with this attitude of the Bohemian reformation, our peace work has developed in recent years. It is significant that we keep this matter before our eyes in order to be able to understand our peace work as it is embodied particularly in the work of the Christian Peace Conference. We encounter many hesitations and suspicions against this work. In the last resort, is it not an opportunistic work, even if undertaken perhaps with a certain subjective honesty? Is it not impelled by an equivocal theology of basically nontheological, alien loyalties? We listen to these questions, and we cannot refute them at the outset in a sure-of-ourselves and self-justified manner. They call us to question ourselves and to reflect in the "community of pilgrims." But right there a clear continuity with our fathers, understanding the peace mission of the church as its fundamental obligation, helps us to understand our peace work not as some fashionable *allotrion* (alien, inappropriate matter) that was imported from the outside, but as our genuine task. In our decision-making today, where we meet the incomparably heightened dangers of the atomic era, we yet stand in the community of faith with our forefathers and brothers. Thus also in this respect the historical background of our theological and churchly existence becomes our sustaining ground.

How has this sustaining ground of the theological insights of the Czech reformation helped our churches in meeting the challenge of our socialist society?

THE CHURCH
IN A SOCIALIST SOCIETY

THE FACE
OF A SOCIALIST SOCIETY

Our world has changed. This is a universal experience that—in the face of technological and social revolutions of our times—is being felt and expressed by Christians in almost the entire ecumenical world. In a radical way such change applies to the churches in the socialist countries, who in recent decades have gone through a revolutionary transformation of their secular order. The changes are far-reaching and almost unprecedented; their main emphasis has been in the economic, political, and cultural fields; their aim is reconstruction toward a socialist society.

Economically, this means a real revolution in the management of national and social resources. The means of production were socialized. Their ownership was transferred from private hands to the state or to communities. The power of private capital, of "big business" and "big finance," was eliminated. In Czechoslovakia, this was carried through with exceptional radicality. Not only key industries and banks were nationalized, but virtually all branches of industry, commerce, and services. Whereas in other socialist countries some space was left for limited private activity and ownership of industry (as in the German Democratic Republic) or agriculture (as in Poland), in Czechoslovakia all levels of economic life became socialized, including the decisive realm of agriculture. With the exception of some farmers, some old handworkers, and some artists, there is no group of people and no profession which would be considered "private." No wonder, then, that the Comumnist Party of Czechoslovakia asserted the adoption of the predicate "socialist" into the official name of the Republic: Czechoslovak Socialist Republic. Czechoslovakia was so declared the first socialist state after the Soviet Union. This was more than a formal solemn act. The establishment of a socialist economic order was certainly not without problems, especially for people who got under the wheels of the socialist revolution. Still more difficult was the task of developing the socialist economy into an effective and efficient system overcoming a certain tendency toward a bureaucratic rigidity in its management. Serious symptoms of stagnation within the Czechoslovak economy indicated the difficulties of our endeavors. The call for radical economic reform became nearly general. Yet in all this, the call and the program was for reform of a *socialist* economy, not a return to capitalism. As far as the great majority of citizens was concerned, the basic validity of a socialist order was never questioned.

This radical economic change was achieved by a revolutionary overthrow of the *political* structure, namely, by the concentration of all decisive political power in the Communist Party. This happened in February, 1948. In a serious crisis within the Czechoslovak socialist democracy, the Communists used their decisive power-political position as the strongest political party (more than 40 percent of the popular vote in democratic elections in 1946) to take over the government of the country. The system evolved in the next years was not theoretically a one-party system. Four other parties remained (two in the Czech part of the country and two in Slovakia). Yet the possibilities of those four parties were strictly limited, as were (up to 1968) the possibilities of other organized bodies, such as the trade unions. All these political organizations were part of the National Front, and this body was both theoretically and practically under the firm leadership of the Party. Thus Czechoslovakia of the fifties and sixties emerged as a rather monolithic and highly centralized political structure.

The ideological basis for this development was the doctrine of the "dictatorship of the proletariat." This is an important Marxist concept. In its original context it is conceived as an emergency instrument of revolutionary change. As such it is meaningful. It becomes, however, ambiguous and dangerous if "eternalized," that is, identified with a certain institution and its policy. For then the concentration of power, which may be provisionally necessary, tends to absolutize its given structure. This temptation became clearly visible in the years of Stalinism and its "cult of personality," when citizens of the socialist country became very often objects rather than subjects of political decisions—of some good political decisions, to be sure, but also of wrong decisions, and without effective control of them. The political trials in Czechoslovakia of the early fifties were symptomatic of this tendency. Some of these processes were really created out of nothing; in this sense, they were acts of arbitrary, omnipotent, cultically absolutized personalities. The result was alienation, especially of the younger generation, from political participation, and a prevailing mood of political apathy, so typical in the greater part of the Novotný era. The revolutionary breakthrough of the Czechoslovak spring of 1968 is to be understood and interpreted against this background.

The emphasis on centralized political power implied an emphasis on a centralized *cultural policy*. Monopoly of power tended toward monopoly of truth. The aim of this policy was the cultural revolution, the radical change of the public consciousness, and the realization of a new socialist humanity. The writers, artists, and teachers were encouraged to act as "engineers of human souls." This yielded important positive results. Broad possibilities of a highly developed educational system became accessible also to those once underprivileged in this area, especially the workers. At the same time, the socialist economy provided a strong base for artistic development—for example, the considerable progress of the Czechoslovak film would have been hardly possible without the structural changes in the organization of the nationalized film industry.

Yet realization exactly of these educational and artistic possibilities often developed in tension with a too rigid conception of the cultural revolution. Thus, much of creative new art emerged on a socialist basis to champion concrete individual humanity against the rigid system of cultural manipulation. Very often this art defied the stereotypes of the official "socialist realism" (which proved to be generally rather more idealistic than realistic, enforcing ideological clichés of human reality). This ferment among writers and artists, students and scientists, became one of the most persistent impulses toward the effective democratization of socialist society in the later sixties.

Already these deep changes in the economic, political, and cultural system of the country implied a radical challenge to Christian churches. Both the positive elimination of some of the gravest social injustices within traditional class societies and the dangers of a centralized monopoly of political power considerably changed the conditions of men. The church had to respond to them—not just in solemn declarations but in all its preaching, teaching, and pastoral care. Many traditional categories and attitudes —especially in Christian social ethics—required rethinking. Many prevailing presuppositions of middle-class morality were evidently questioned (for instance, the role of private property): Should they be defended at all cost, or should the theologians rather examine our conscious and subconscious prejudices in the light of the biblical vision in order to gain a new freedom not only *in* the new society but also *for* that society?

The challenge to the churches soon also became direct. The socialist revolution affected not only the economic, social, and cultural realms but also the place and life of the churches. The reconstruction of society was based on clearly defined presuppositions of an ideology claiming to be the sole authority in all the essential public spheres. This was the ideology of Marxism-Leninism, an ideology programmatically materialistic and atheistic. Sharp criticism of the churches and religion is a fundamental, persistent Marxist tradition. Thus the concept of a cultural revolution entailed the task of overcoming religion. For a socialist man, religious practice is a sign of imperfection. This was strongly emphasized with respect to the Party members. Sometimes, however, this attitude has been extended also to people outside the Party, especially if they were in leading positions. For example, when the movement of Socialist Brigades (selected groups of people of exemplary socialist conduct in work and life) was organized in Czechoslovakia, there were hesitations as to whether practicing Christians could be accepted into those core groups of socialist humanity, even when they otherwise fulfilled all standards for acceptance. Allegiance to a church was understood as a lack of socialist consciousness. A truly socialist man had to "settle the religious problem" first (i.e., break with the churches). Thus anti-religious propaganda (though never very effective and hardly a serious problem for most Christians) became a part of the official cultural activities.

This negative attitude toward religion did not necessarily imply direct repressive measures against the churches. In the classic Marxist tradition, religion is not simply the root of all the social evils (as some of the bourgeois radicals of European free thought often argued); rather, it is an expression of that really radical evil which is the unjust social order. Thus, an authentic Marxism never considers repression a legitimate way of "solving" the problem of religion. Whenever such measures appear they are detrimental not only to the religious community but also to Marxist society (as is the case also, by the way, with Christian churches when tempted to use repressive measures against their dissidents or opponents). This restraint helped to keep open a space of practical tolerance for religious communities in our socialist society. The width of that area was often a matter of dispute between the representatives of the state and of the churches. It was often narrowed down, yet it was never destroyed.

A constitutional basis for such coexistence was already provided in 1949 by the laws concerning economic assistance to the churches. The idea of public economic contributions to religious bodies is certainly puzzling from the point of view of American culture, with its tradition of separation between the church and the state. It is to be understood only against a background of age-long European tradition (prevalent especially in the Catholic countries) and, of course, in the specific situation in Czechoslovakia after 1948. The property of the churches was to a high degree nationalized in the course of the socialist revolution. Nationalization especially affected the Roman Catholic Church (other churches had no considerable property). It was, therefore, the position of this church which was mainly considered in the church laws of 1949; economic assistance to the churches (consisting basically of paid state salaries for ministers and priests) was a compensation for the socialized church property.

The church laws of 1949 reflect a certain continuity within the European tradition of church-state relations. And yet, on the other hand, the socialist revolution represents a radical discontinuity in the situation of the churches within their society and culture. Let us recapitulate: Culture in a Marxist society is not ideologically neutral. It is based on an ideology highly critical of religion and churches. If the whole culture, and especially all public education, is then to be shaped in accord with that ideology, the cultural setting for the churches must change radically. For the first time in centuries, the churches in central Europe lost the privilege of established cultural and social support. For the first time they had to face an ideological climate in their environment that was neither officially benevolent nor neutral but clearly critical and adverse.

THE END OF
THE CONSTANTINIAN ERA

How were we to grasp and interpret this change in the secular order, and how were we to respond to it? In our attempts to conceptualize the situation, we frequently used an almost notorious slogan: "We have come to the end of the Constantinian era." What was meant by that?

By the "Constantinian era" we mean the epoch of powerful Christendom (*corpus christianum*), of the political and cultural power of Christianity, of "Christian civilization." In its most outspoken form, it was the epoch of concordats between state and church, an arrangement whereby the church was either patronized by the state or at least protected, and where the state was regarded by the church as *defensor fidei* and exalted by her. For centuries Christendom in Europe belonged to this epoch and received its distinctive character—even in the depths and heights of its theological and ecclesiastical existence—through all the typical facets of this epoch. Christendom built its historic house in this epoch, dwelt in it, and got accustomed to it. The churches of the Reformation did indeed fundamentally rebuild it—but nothing more. They too, apart from the radical movements which have always remained a small minority, firmly maintained its foundations. This applies, in a more subtle form, even to the American situation. In spite of the separation between church and state (a positive American tradition) churches enjoy clear privileges within the established society and culture (tax and draft exemptions, large educational institutions, respect paid by vote-seeking politicians, etc.).

As far as men can judge, this era, covering nearly the whole of church history until now, is at an end for us. The residue of the Constantinian order still survives into the socialist epoch; the weight of a thousand years of European history still makes itself felt in it. One example is the fact, just mentioned, that in the Czechoslovak Socialist Republic the church still receives financial support from the Marxist state; another would be the cultural and historical context in which certain decidedly Christian movements and traditions of the past—as, for example, the Hussite movement—are maintained by public opinion even in a society that is avowedly atheist. In all essentials, however, the Constantinian solution for the relationship between church and state is over. The church is no longer one of the official pillars of society. The opposite, rather, is true: in the context of the fundamental aspirations of this society the church is ultimately regarded as a relic of a past epoch; for pragmatic political reasons it is to be tolerated, but it (at least in its original, religious form) is intrinsically foreign to the future of a socialist society. The individual Christian as such is no longer protected and privileged by his society; his public prestige is not increased on account of his being a Christian; he no longer conforms to a desirable rule but is, rather, an exception, not the householder but a stranger and sojourner within his culture.

At this point the urgent question arises: How is the church to react to this deep change in the temporal order? This question has confronted our congregations most urgently in recent decades—both in the context of the problem of a fundamental theological orientation and in respect to the important practical question of the proper function of a church in the new society. How shall this question be answered?

TWO TEMPTATIONS
CONFRONTING THE CHURCH

I cannot present any fixed solution or clear-cut answer to these questions. If I were to sum up some of our experiences and reflections in a tentative attempt to outline a certain field for viable answers, however, I would draw two lines suggesting two impossible possibilities, two blind alleys, on the path of a church in its socialist society. In our search toward a responsible theological orientation, two more or less clearly opposite temptations emerge:

1. There is the danger that, faced with the radicality of change, we might be overcome by a spell of theological

giddiness. By this I mean that we could lose theological sovereignty and simply tailor the gospel to the new situation and ideology. Confronted with this temptation, we should not be too ready to assume a self-righteous attitude. This, after all, has been the notorious danger to the church throughout the whole course of its history. It has always been tempted to adapt itself to its surroundings. One look at church history will confirm that fact. Consider the extent to which Christianity in the feudal age became feudalized—even to the most subtle problems of theology! And how often in the bourgeois epoch Christianity became simply—bourgeois! Why, then, in a socialist epoch, should a "socialist Christianity" not come into being? Why do people only then, as so frequently happens, get frightened and sound the alarm? Yet adaptation is, and remains, a temptation.

2. But there is the opposite danger: the temptation to say a clear-cut no to this development, to see the threat to the Constantinian era simply as a threat to the cause of Jesus Christ and consequently to oppose this development to a greater or lesser degree. This temptation is, so to speak, natural, particularly for the Roman Catholic Church, or at least for her conservative wing, for whom rejection of the Christian (and this generally means the medieval-feudal) civilization often seems identical with rejection of Jesus Christ. But other Christian churches—including the churches of the Reformation—are equally faced with this temptation, especially when a form of society as clearly defined as the Marxist society replaces the Constantinian society.

Both these possible positions are theologically false, and for a faithful church they are indeed impossible. The error of the former position is obvious: using the important formulation of the Confession of Barmen (of the

German Confessional Church in 1934), which in its marvelous actuality proved to be a prophetically testing and strengthening word in our situation too, the "one Word of God" is made a relative entity with which other historical entities are fused and confused. The Word of God loses its sovereignty; it is made to conform.

The error of the other position is less obvious, yet it is—in spite of the opposed practical attitude—surprisingly akin to the error of the former position: for here too the one Word of God is, in a similar way, associated with a historical entity, this time perhaps an ecclesiastical one, yet, even so, an entity no less relative and historical. This is the temptation to identify "Christian civilization" with the cause of Jesus Christ. Such an identification then necessarily implies a negative attitude in the face of the threat of the Constantinian epoch. Here, too, one becomes a victim to human and historical prejudices. Here, too, God's word loses its sovereignty and becomes conformable.

Both these positions are therefore equally impossible. Both ways lead astray. Both are to be avoided. Yet as soon as we leave the level of principles and turn toward actual Christian existence, it is necessary to add that these temptations have not been equally real or equally dangerous. The first temptation is relatively weak, both in the ecumenical world and with us. The temptation to assimilate the church to the post-Constantinian order, particularly in its most pronounced form of a socialist Christianity, an ideological blending of Marxism with the gospel, is only slight. Neither the church nor the Marxist state encourages it. We may say, perhaps, that the changed climate of post-Constantinian society in regard to religion—for example, the atheism of Marxist ideology—in a way benefits Christian existence in the socialist system. The danger of an ideological assimilation on the part of the church is undoubtedly less than if it were confronted by a religious or idealist state ideology.

The second temptation, on the other hand, is much greater—and for the same reason: faced with atheism, the church is being tempted by its own presuppositions and principles to assume a hostile attitude, then to extend this hostility to other components of the system, especially when they are not to the taste of its traditional bourgeois position.

It has been the task of our theological work to withstand precisely this second "reactionary" temptation—without losing sight of the first. This has been done mainly through the pioneering work of J. L. Hromádka. His creative "one-sidedness"—frequently misunderstood and criticized in the ecumenical world—must be understood precisely in this connection: as an attempt to defend the freedom of the church against the temptation of an unfruitful negativism in the light of the revolutionary breakup of the Constantinian order. We attempted this—in the context of the ecumenical biblical theological renewal chiefly represented by the theology of Karl Barth—by a return to the foundations of the biblical message.

At the same time—and with growing intensity within the church, in some respects even within the nation—the historical context of our reformation grew very relevant. Let me suggest this helpful presence of our spiritual heritage by recalling some of those theological accents of the Czech reformation which we treated in the preceding chapter.

1. *An evangelical obedience under the Lordship of Christ.* What inspiration comes with this fundamental emphasis to the community at the end of the Constantinian era! Jesus Christ is the Lord! (a) He is the only

Lord of his community. There is no situation in which he will not be present with us, no situation in which we will be abandoned and forsaken. (b) Furthermore, he is the Lord of the world. There is no worldly order to which he will be bound, no worldly order by whose transformation his presence will be endangered. In this sense there is no atheistic world, one really abandoned by God. (c) And he is the Lord of the future. With its eyes fastened on him, the church may go forth in hope even when it steps out into unknown and formerly untried pathways. His promise is valid even if the church of the post-Constantinian era must leave a historical house in which it has lived for centuries. It need not be crippled in its eviction.

2. *The church of the martyrs*. We have seen what that meant in the understanding of the Bohemian reformation. (a) The church is a fellowship of pilgrims, a community which knows that it can have its earthly rest in no part of this world. It knows that it is unfaithful if it settles down in any historic situation. It knows that it is always on the road, that it must no longer cast its glance backward, but always forward. (b) It is the brotherhood of servants, a community that knows that the proper form for the community of Jesus is not the form of overlordship and majestic institution but the form of a serving community. Consequently, the Constantinian church form, in the light of the gospel, is in no way the only possible or promised and promising mode of its being. Rather, the opposite is true. The Constantinian church appears in many respects as a rather problematic form of being. Even within an undisturbed Constantinian era, Petr Chelčický, a great Hussite layman of the early fifteenth century, set forth this idea in an exceptional way. He understood the Constantinian alliance as the great temptation and the original sin of historic Christendom. Two monstrous whales—the

pope and the emperor—have chewed up the apostolic net of faith in their alliance since 313. In Chelčický's perspective, the end of the Constantinian era could not appear merely as a disaster but also as a real opportunity. Therefore, the post-Constantinian church need not merely weep over lost opportunities; rather, it can imaginatively and joyfully seek and use the possibilities still present and, especially, those newly open. (c) The church is the community of debtors. As such, it cannot see the world simply as an object to be "Christianized"; on the contrary, it views the world as an object of God's love. To bear witness to that love of God toward the world—to its pious ones as well as to its godless ones—is the only fundamental debt of the Christian church. This mission is not at the end in a situation in which the secularized society revolts against the Constantinian privileges of the churches. The debt of the apostolic mission remains open even when the church falters, when the church of witnesses becomes in the deepest sense the church of martyrs —and with this debt also remains open the real future of the church. The post-Constantinian church stands beneath the cross, but it stands also in the light of the resurrection.

3. *The church of the people.* I have emphasized that the Hussites and the Brethren understood the gospel in its prophetic and evangelic orientation toward the weary and heavy-laden, the oppressed and belabored. Consequently, they interpreted it in a revolutionary way. That helps us to find an open-minded attitude toward our socialist society. On the basis of the historical background of the Hussite reformation we regard the socialist movement as a part of *our* history. Our socialist friends regard our reformation as a portion of their own prehistory. This "common ground" does not imply any ideological fusion. In this respect we consider ourselves as a free

church—a pilgrim church under the Lordship of Jesus also in this respect. Yet "free church" means at the same time a church without prejudices, open for positive possibilities of its society, a church of "proexistence," seeking what is good "for the city." As a church of the people we are a church of *this* people, *this* society.

All these tentative reflections offer a fundamental assurance for the church's road into the post-Constantinian society: *This way is open.* The mission continues. The service is being done. It is not superfluous to stress this statement, for faith is not stating an obvious truth here. Even in our congregations, faced with an estranged and secularized environment, people have been often heard asking: Has the church any future at all? And in our ecumenical relationships we are obliged to listen to the questions so frequently raised by Christians who live under different and still largely Constantinian conditions: Can the church exist at all in a fundamentally atheist society? And can it faithfully discharge its commission in that society?

One slogan emerges frequently in this connection: the slogan of *totalitarianism.* The doubts concerning the possibilities of the socialist society, and especially the possibilities of the Christian witness in it, are often justified by referring to socialism's "totalitarian tendencies." We cannot discuss the full problem of totalitarianism in this context. Sometimes this term has been used simply as a tool of Cold War propaganda to support the argument that Communism and Fascism are only two branches of the same totalitarian tree. We emphatically reject this argument. There is a basic difference between Communism, with its constructive and humanistic possibilities, and destructive and nihilistic Fascism.

Yet the term "totalitarian" can be used in a more sober and less biased way, in denoting the tendency of a society to proclaim one ideology—and possibly one political party —as the only legitimate power within that society. We cannot deny that such a tendency exists in our society and that it poses serious human problems, especially for those people who profess a different ideology—for example, Christians within a Marxist society. Still the problem should not be exaggerated and metaphysically absolutized. There are two basic reasons for this warning:

1. An ideology is never the whole of human reality. It is an important and influential—therefore by no means indifferent—element of social life. But the real life of men is always much richer and more complex than its ideological pattern. Concretely, an atheistic ideological program does not create an atheistic society, just as a Christian program does not create a Christian society.

2. A socialist society is by no means a static society; it is rather a dynamic society. It may have had its days of rigidity, and some more may still come, yet the creative changes are not only a possibility but a decisive reality, bringing with them a growing range of responsible participation and effective social action. To see the basic situation of man—and the situation of the church—in this society as captured within a "totalitarian structure" is totally inadequate.

From this pragmatic point of view, skeptical doubts about the possibility of a Christian existence and mission in a socialist society are not justified, and from the *theological* point of view, they must be dismissed, recalling the fundamental biblical assurance. In the light of this promise, such doubts may frequently manifest a spiritual inertia that, consciously or unconsciously, links the cause of Christ with a historical Constantinian opportunity, incapable of thinking imaginatively of the creative possibilities of the Holy Spirit; they may even reflect traces of a certain latent "atheism," which does not take seriously the sovereign freedom of God. That is why, in answering these well-meant but sometimes slightly petulant questions, we say emphatically, as Christians in a socialist society: The way remains open, the mission continues, the service is being fulfilled. No false cares—the cares of unbelief! Rather, the true care of faith. How, in fact, are we to go this way and walk in it straight and upright? How may the church in our society serve in obedience, and what is it to do? To this question we now turn.

A "CIVILIAN PROCLAMATION"

I shall try to consider some of the thinking and reasoning about the church's witness in the post-Constantinian society, which in our actual situation is a Marxist-socialist one, under the motto "civilian proclamation" (*zivile Verkündigung*). This motto has been coined in our congregations during recent years of intensive inquiry into a more credible and effective way of service for our church. In English it sounds slightly enigmatic. It points in a direction similar to the ecumenically inspiring program of "nonreligious interpretation" of Dietrich Bonhoeffer, with the difference that with us the ethical-social component rather than the hermeneutical is in the foreground. We try to denote by it the search for new ways for the church's witness in a world that, on account of the general secularization and its official ideological basis, has to a large extent become estranged from the church, so that the customary Constantinian opportunities—like the customary media of mass evangelization—have become spiritually as well as technically inadequate. The motto itself is of no importance. We use it merely because it contains many shades of meaning and thus brings out graphically some of the implications with which we have been concerned.

Let us spell out the program of a "civilian proclamation," particularly as regards its consequences for the church's function in society with the following three points: (1) proving the freedom of the gospel: reducing traditional "uniforms" (rules of life); (2) serving in the movement from the church toward the world: the way of an excentric congregation; (3) witnessing in interhuman relations: an unconditional humanism.

1. We begin with the external, almost banal, aspect of civilian witness, which, however, has a certain significance because it is the presupposition of Christian service in a society in which traditional ecclesiastical forms and institutions are no longer socially relevant. There is, first, a *civilian mode of life* for Christians—a *witness without religious uniform,* "without long robes," without the traditional solemn ecclesiastical dress. In many people's minds Christianity—as one looks back to the Constantinian form of the church—is at first related to a certain dress, a "uniform" in the sense of a distinct mode of life. Thus, Christianity may be understood, for example, as an institute for cultivating religious-liturgical or ascetic

laws and customs. To be a Christian, then, implies taking part in religious ceremonies, liturgical actions, pious usages, or self-denying exercises. Or one may interpret Christian faith in a moralistic, puritanical sense: "The Christian does not smoke or drink or dance. . . ." Or, again, Christianity may be assigned to cultural-political categories: to be a Christian is to belong to a certain party, generally a party of the pious against the "godless."

The Christian church bears much blame for these misinterpretations. In the course of its history it has seen itself in these uniforms and shown itself in them to Christians and non-Christians alike. How often the church has succumbed to the temptation to understand itself or to let itself be understood as a religious institute, a society for the cultivation of a religious style of life! In this way all kinds of prejudices were implanted and developed, so that the good news of the gospel became identified with religion. This was the case both in the minds of its friends and then, consequently, in the minds of its foes. This, particularly, may have been the danger of the Roman Catholic religion. But Protestant churches too, for their part, have cultivated distinct, if somewhat different, prejudices. We may think, for instance, of the puritanical uniform so dear to the Reformed (Calvinist) or the pietistic type of the Reformation. Allegiance to Jesus Christ was frequently mistaken for allegiance to a puritanical-moralistic style of life. And do not large numbers of Christians today—both Roman Catholic and Protestant —fall victim to the third form of misunderstanding by linking Christianity with the cause of a distinct civilization—that, for instance, of the "Christian Occident"?

In all these uniforms a terrible temptation assails the church: the gospel of the free grace of God becomes a law; the redemption of the whole of life becomes a fragment of life; salvation for all becomes salvation only for those who are near, which in turn is all too easily misunderstood as condemnation for those who are far off. The result is a separation that is bad because it is superficial, self-chosen, not justified by the gospel. Thus, the gospel is considerably reduced. There are, admittedly, many and diverse laws of human behavior and style. Many of these laws also apply to Christians and control their lives. But the gospel must on no account be confused with these laws, for it is not they which characterize and distinguish the Christian. The distinctiveness of the Christian is not a program which could be realized through these outward means. It goes much deeper; it is rooted not in a style of life but in faith itself.

"Civilian proclamation" attempts to withstand these temptations to legalize or to make wrong distinctions. It tries to lead congregations away from cultivating a certain style, a "Christian manner," a code of conduct, from being different on principle, and to lead them to what is simply human, natural, even worldly. The Christian is first and foremost simply a man, a man of his age, a man among men. And today this means: a modern man. He is not fundamentally different from others. "To the Jews he is like a Jew, and to the Greeks like a Greek." He does not live a deliberately distinct existence. In his "dress," that is, in his style of life—the outward forms of his demeanor, his interests—he is a man of his time. He is not a keeper of ancient monuments, not an exponent of the Middle Ages. He is not a person who on principle always draws lines and guards them—one who is always different, a man whose heart beats to a rhythm different from that of his fellowmen. On the contrary, he is, in the full meaning of the phrase, a "*con*temporary," a man among men—a *civilian*.

This civilian way of the Christian is certainly not an

end in itself and not the last word. In itself it is not the testimony but a means of promoting it: the civilian man is now being called to bear witness to Jesus Christ. He stands where his neighbors stand, but he stands there as one who tries to remain faithful to his Lord. Here, then, begins the way of the Christian—in following Jesus, in believing, hoping, and loving. In the midst of unbelief, faith. In the midst of despair, hope. In the midst of hatred, love. When this is happening, the true distinction and the real witness come to pass, yet not through any self-chosen differentiation but through the fundamental direction of existence. To guard this direction, to defend it from shallow legal limitations, and to distinguish the true witness to Jesus Christ from the substitute wares of a religious style of life is the intention of the "civilian proclamation" as implied in our motto.

At a time of social change, when a certain social order (a "law") is being replaced by another, this proclamation may be of particular significance. At such a moment there looms the danger of the church's being identified with the "old law." The church appears to be the exponent of the past order, and the gospel is seen as the ideology of the former society. And even worse, the church is tempted to understand itself within these categories. This is attractive because at first it seems promising; some people join the church for cryptopolitical reasons and out of resentment. And yet every step in this direction is fateful, for it endangers the true witness of the gospel—and makes it particularly inaccessible to the representatives of the new society. This is the point at which, for example, the theology of anti-Communism becomes disastrous: it turns the free gospel—which must also be understood as the gospel for atheists—into a law of bondage. Thus, in striving after a "civilian proclamation," we seek to maintain the freedom of the gospel in the very age of social change.

2. Here the second dimension of the worldly testimony becomes evident: evangelical service within a worldly, social, and therefore civilian life. We understand this service not merely in the demand for decent behavior as a citizen —which is also important. But more is at stake in this aspect of civilian proclamation: an understanding of and witnessing to the gospel in its movement *from the church to the world,* the direction of the Christian life which corresponds to this encounter.

Movement from church to world: from the point of view of the church this may seem dubious. Do not these words suggest precisely a program of secularization, eliminating the influence of the church from one department of public life after another? Of course we have to distinguish. There is a theologically exaggerated version of the movement from the church to the world—if this is understood to mean the merging of the church into the state, or if a thoroughly justified criticism of ecclesiastical institutions is magnified into a desire to destroy these institutions. This almost appears to be a Manichaean attitude. The historical burden—and the historical guilt—of ecclesiastical institutions is immense. But the institutional aspect of church life is not only a menace but also a need and a necessity: life in the flesh—in history—also needs this support of spiritual life.

And yet the movement from the church to the world is a legitimate path for the church—and its duty. Perhaps the process of secularization from the church to the world is but a response to the guilt which the church itself has committed by notoriously curtailing its movement toward the world. Church history is full of evidence. Again and again the church has yielded to the temptation to replace the legitimate route of its service—and this is what matters—by one in the opposite direction: from the world to the church. Such a movement assumed different forms: the form of a domineering clericalism in its Roman-medieval version or in the Protestant-modern version of a "purple church." The tendency was also at work in much more subtle, more spiritual guises—even within the structure of the church's work. We see it, for example, in the customary exaltation of Sunday over the working day, the unquestioning concentration of attention almost exclusively on solemn, festal, religious occasions; in the suggested superiority of the priest over the layman, which, in spite of Reformation principles, keeps its ground even in the Evangelical churches—at least in the form of a questionable sovereignty of the religious "professional" over the "amateur" (or in the minister's one-sided claim on the laity's interest without, as a rule, an equivalent interest on his part in questions which occupy the layman). This is in line with typically religious attitudes: a hierarchical movement in worship, in theology, in social structure. The priest likes to be at the head of the community: *Ecclesia praecedit.* The movement of the gospel—as embodied in Jesus Christ—is diametrically opposed to this typical movement of religion. According to Philippians 2:5–11 service, sacrifice, solidarity, are what matter. In this movement the church is being constituted not as an autocratic institution but as an excentric community, a community, that is, which does not have its center within itself. The paradigm of its discipleship is from the church to the world.

A "civilian interpretation" tries to do justice to this movement. It stresses the theological honor of the working day. This does not detract from the true sovereignty of Sunday, the "Lord's Day." But this day is indissolubly linked with the "working days": "The sabbath was made for man, and not man for the sabbath" (Mark 2:27). A church which remains true to its constitutive movement can therefore never be content to be the church of a single day. It will always claim the whole week. The theme of the weekday must also be taken much more seriously in the liturgical activity of the church, so that its worship does not become a sacred reserve but an offering in dedication to the world, to the actual joys and sorrows, labor and suffering, of man. And this applies also to the scope of parochial life. The purpose of the Christian congregation—particularly of the churches of the Reformation to which it was committed as a special *charisma* and a special obligation—is to grow not merely into a ghettolike community centered on a cult but into a community of all life, into a fellowship that prays, works, and suffers together.

This implies a much more serious participation of the laity in the work, for when the church understands itself in this way, it becomes obvious that the church is maintained not only by the clergy but by every member. Indeed, when the movement from the church to the world is taken seriously, it is precisely the layman who becomes the true exponent of this legitimate movement. It is precisely the revolutionary changes of the Constantinian order which make it unambiguously clear that the laity constitutes the proper "apostolic existence" of the church of Jesus Christ in the post-Constantinian world.

And the movement involves not only the layman. The atheist, estranged from the church, is also involved within the true movement from the church to the world. In a certain sense even those who perhaps have never set foot on the floor of the church belong to its sphere—the sphere of its prayer and its work. They, too, should be its concern, even in their absence—and perhaps for that very reason. They, too, have the right to have their say even as regards the sermon—they, too, should be included in its message, and not merely as the "dark background" of the lost from whom those present in church are so nicely set apart as children of light from the children of darkness (how often the church has preached this way— and still does!) but as those with whom we are united in sin and in hope through Jesus Christ. Thus the world becomes present in the church—and the church in the world.

Civilian testimony has not only a human and individual dimension but also a social and collective one. Ultimately our service is concerned with real persons. But the development of modern society has shown with absolute clarity that no real persons exist without wider social relationships. Such relations—in particular the economic and political—therefore concern the church, which cannot practice political abstinence and offer as a reason for it that "the political song is a nasty song." The church has to join in singing this song—with a genuine and pure intent in the light of the gospel, without any opportunism or resentment of the prevailing fashion. Then this song— concern for better justice, truer freedom, and a really just peace of the world—is part of the divine service. And inversely, the divine service—the perspective of the gospel —belongs to the center of life in society in the civilian expression of faith.

This civilian participation of the church in the life of the world forms an important basis for a credible witness. It seems that only from this serving presence in the world, from an undemanding engagement of Christians in the burning problems of the time, can a witness evolve which makes one's neighbors prick up their ears. At a time of immense inflation of all words through the mass media of advertising and propaganda, the mere religious word is more powerless than ever. And the same may well apply to the customary means of mass evangelization and mission, even if from time to time their success—apparent or real?—is great. Mature, worldly men will hardly be reached by these methods. A credible testimony will develop only from the depth of real life, not hastily and superficially. In this sense a true civilian mode is a prerequisite of Christian witness in the modern world.

And it is not only a prerequisite. In a sense this civilian presence in the world is already witnessing—even if it is not yet considered or labeled as such. Dedication to the world in following God's way to men is meaningful in itself—quite apart from any results achieved by the church's standards. "Results and successes" in the church's activity are, of course, by no means a matter for indifference. The missionary point of view in the church is justified. But it is not the only point of view—not even the first or the last one. Only service itself ranks so high. We do well to remember this in regard to the church's activity— also in regard to new ways of this activity, for example, the attempts at a civilian proclamation. These experiments might also be understood as another "new strategy," or "method," as a clerical "gimmick"—as the last attempt of the church to conquer "its" world. Some of the new ways of the church's work could be so interpreted. But this is ultimately a misunderstanding—and no true help for the church or for the world. For the promise of Jesus Christ to the church is given only in the way of guileless, simple service. A genuine turning of the church to the world will be based not on clever calculations but on following the way of Jesus. Only by following him can the true dimension of a civilian witness be perceived and faith be tested in the world.

3. We come now to the third "level" of the church's civilian service in our society: witnessing to the gospel in interhuman relations, striving after an *evangelical pro-*

existence. It was mainly in this sense that our congregations understood the concept of "civilian interpretation" as one of the most urgent tasks and as one of the opportunities for Christian service in our society. And rightly so, for the quest for the neighbor is one of the most burning questions of our time. To be sure, this question is an ancient human issue, one of the few basic questions of man. Today, however, it is being asked with particular urgency. This urgency is implicit in the structure of modern living, in the rise of technical civilization, of mass society in the world. The Christian need not deplore this development. He knows soberly that it has unlocked unheard-of possibilities and realities for man. Foundations have been laid for effectively overcoming some of the fundamental evils of past epochs; we cannot sufficiently stress what it means that from large parts of the world hunger, epidemics, and unemployment have disappeared and are still disappearing. We have much reason to be proud of our present age. Yet it, too, has its dangers and troubles. And one of its deepest needs is the need of man for his fellowman. Amid the incalculable entities and numbers of this technical civilization and its mass society, man is always in danger of becoming a cog in a vast machine, of representing a function rather than a person. He is easily ignored as a personality. Lonely people in the human masses of great cities, men forsaken by the welfare state, neighbors in close physical proximity unknown to one another—these situations are well known. Within them, man is in danger of losing much that is essential: personal relations, mutual understanding and interest, individual assistance. Man's hunger for personal humanity, for one's fellowmen, is not being satisfied.

Here, then, is an important opening for the civilian testimony of a Christian in the modern world. Precisely here he is called, even demanded, with particular urgency. The gospel itself sends him on this way, the way of fellow humanity, for ultimately the gospel is God's search for man. We need but to recall the hymnological summary of Christ's way in Philippians 2 with its key sentence "and was made in the likeness of men," or the saying in Titus of the appearing of the "love of God toward man" (3:4). And we may remember Matthew 25:40, in which, following this "divine humanism," men's turning toward their neighbors is made the touchstone of their Christian faith: "Inasmuch as ye have done it unto one of the least of my brethren, ye have done it unto me." Here the scope of the Christian witness is indicated: proexistence, existence for others. Only in this movement toward one's neighbor can Jesus Christ be obediently followed; only in this movement can we tread the Christian way.

This way, then, leads to unconditional humanity. I emphasize the "unconditional" of man's turning to his neighbor, for it is here that Christian humanism is distinguished from general philanthropy. We appreciate secular forms of solidarity with men in the numerous humanist efforts of our days. We gratefully share part of the way in common with these efforts. At times we are put to shame by the resolve and willingness on the part of non-Christians to make sacrifices in this cause. We do not separate from them prematurely and rashly. And yet there is a legitimate parting of the ways. Current humanism is all too fond of drawing lines. Its first and often exclusive concern is for the "neighbor" in the literal sense of the word: for him who is nigh, for those who belong to the same nation, race, class, or religion. Sooner or later the open windows are shut. But the Christian is called to his fellowman even when every natural or ideological sympathy has ceased; when he can no longer see any natural or historic reason for it; where only walls or chasms of traditional enmity may be discerned. It is difficult indeed to demonstrate true humanity under such circumstances. But this, precisely, is the mission of the Christian: to seek and see the face of Jesus Christ over every man. There is a beautiful saying by Luther: "to receive Jesus Christ in every man and to be Jesus Christ to every man." This means that for the sake of Jesus Christ none may ever be excluded from our common humanity. To look for this bond even when defending ourselves, when contradicting, when facing the opponent—and to love even the enemy—this is the Christian witness.

Let us finally mention two examples and results of this unconditional Christian service within the framework of human relations. From the start Christian solidarity has tended with particular devotion after those for whom nobody cared, the poor and the sick, the forgotten and oppressed, those who from a utilitarian point of view were considered unproductive or superfluous. Let us remember the place of honor in the Old Testament for the "orphans and widows" or in the gospel for those who "labor and are heavy-laden"! At this point both the temptation and the honor of Christian philanthropy arise. I speak of the temptation of philanthropy—the temptation for the church to express its responsibility for man, for the neighbor, exclusively in categories of personal welfare, of charity. This is a harmful limitation of Christian brotherly love. It is a judgment on our faithfulness that a movement outside the church—in particular, socialism—has recognized this shortcoming more clearly than the majority of Christians. To help a person effectively demands a purposeful, organized, and planned system of welfare for the whole sphere of man's social life, a reconstruction of society, not mere treatment of crying individual needs. Here is the reason, based on the gospel, for our saying yes to socialist reconstruction, to its principle, and to many of its results, such as the generous provisions of our health services.

Yet precisely here where the church gratefully acknowledges this national welfare, it will undergird again the honor of philanthropy by its turning to those who need personal understanding, personal care, personal interest, in particular the "orphans and widows" of the modern age—people who are lonely and half-forgotten. Philanthropy in the church—which becomes a stumbling block when it claims to do everything—thus acquires a new meaning where a broad framework of solutions and opportunities has been realized but where the personal turning of man to man is still necessary. "The poor ye have always with you"—a sentence which in the history of the church did much harm because it was understood as a general doctrine of the impossibility and ineffectiveness of social reconstruction—is true here. Here one finds scope for our congregations and for every Christian, scope for a civilian interpretation of the gospel.

The task of civilian interpretation in the sphere of human relations does not, however, end at the level of personal, individual relations. The light of the unconditional philanthropy of God (Titus 3:4) also shines on international relations, that is, on the search for a peaceful order and a greater justice in a world threatened by atomic annihilation. How often has the church at this point hidden its light under a bushel? How often has it strengthened the barriers between nations and power blocs rather than destroyed them? Often it has spiritually justified or even kindled the spirit of the Cold War rather than energetically opposing it. In this sphere Christianity has failed again and again. Yet here there is still an almost unlimited opportunity for new service. Never before, it seems, have we been shown as clearly, now that we are faced with the atomic danger to mankind, that the gospel of God's unconditional will for peace is of direct actuality even in the sphere of "high politics"; there is no other way for the future of mankind than the will for reconciliation and peace. As J. B. Souček puts it: "We can affirm without hesitation that human life cannot continue much longer unless, at critical moments, leading statesmen receive insights that in the last analysis are derived from the Sermon on the Mount. This should both humble the Church and encourage it to be more bold and steadfast in its message to the world."

This is true of other burning issues also. I think especially of the issue of international social justice, of development. As the question of peace and reconciliation became the key issue of ecumenical responsibility in the fifties, so international social justice has become the topic of priority in the sixties. Without a doubt that is today *the* question of a just international order demanding a "revolution of structures" as well as a "revolution of the heart." The "decade of development," as the United Nations hoped the sixties would be, is threatened with disintegration. Conditions in which the undernourished majority of men live have not become better. The disproportion between the developing countries and the industrial ones has grown. And the lethargy on the part of world opinion in relation to the problem of developing countries has also grown. The inertia and provincialism of the industrialized nations dominates their unconcern in this area. Our own socialist society was not an exception in this respect.

Exactly here lies the major responsibility of the churches. Here is another frontier on which to serve with a civilian interpretation of the gospel. If every Sunday in our churches the coming of the Son of God to those close at hand *and* to those far away is preached; if his death and resurrection for all is proclaimed; if, then, the solidarity of the *one* family of mankind, seen in common need and common promise, is made plain, then this must stir a creative unrest for the churches and, through them, for society. Such unrest cannot be satisfied with occasional philanthropy. Instead, it insists continually that the church and the world be brought to a greater justice. It is the task of every church to keep wide open the horizons of that justice and to challenge the notorious parochialism of its environment. The ecumenical experience is of great import in this mission. The witness of brotherly solidarity in a restless, divided world, focused on the rising tensions of these days, is our major chance and a possible contribution. It belongs to the most precious experience in our ecumenical relations of recent years, in Prague, in Geneva in 1966 and in Uppsala in 1968, that again and again we have been able to discover: notwithstanding all weaknesses and all helplessness, a service of reconciliation, the service of peace and justice, is being accomplished in some small degree through our ecumenical work.

Wherever this is done, wherever in torn human relations, of a wider or narrower range, a little island of genuine humanity becomes visible within our churches, there a witness is borne to Jesus Christ, even though he is not expressly named. Witness to Jesus Christ is not borne only where named; it is already borne where the thirsty are given a cup of cold water in his name. His witness works not merely where acknowledged and named as such, where his disciple stands his ground, where he is successful. We are learning afresh that in the biblical term for witness, "martyr," an abiding undertone is discernible. The testimony of Jesus Christ gives light even where its witness seems to fail, where the disciple is not standing his ground, where he is not being recognized and acknowledged, but where he is serving in simple faithfulness to man and thereby to his Lord. Here is "civilian interpretation" in the deepest meaning of this phrase.

CHRISTIANS
IN UNEXPECTED PLACES

What is the sociological basis, the institutional point of departure, for a church's witness in a socialist society? In responding to this question we have to start with a very conventional answer: the basis and point of departure is nothing unexpected; it is the local parish, the congregation. Very common and usual activities of such a parish—Sunday worship, Bible class in the week, the youth group, religious instruction, confirmation—have been and remain the heart of church life.

These old forms of church activity became in a sense

more important than ever before. In our ecumenical exchange today we are critical of the old structures of congregations and sometimes hypercritical of traditional church institutions in general. I agree with much of this criticism. Institutionalism and traditionalism in our churches very often constitute a serious obstacle to all missionary activity and a sound development of free Christian existence. Self-concerned and self-perpetuating institutions sometimes cripple the elementary possibilities of a flexible Christian witness in our secular societies. A living church has to move out from its traditional institutional captivities and seek new ways.

Nevertheless, there are some situations in which even the old forms and the classical institutions acquire a new function and meaning. The situation of the church in a socialist society was one such situation. Under a strong challenge from the outside, the power and the glory of self-concerned church institutions was utterly shaken. Thus the traditional temptations of such institutions diminished. At the same time, their genuine possibility emerged; to once more become modest, functional centers of common Christian life and activity. This was true of many of our local parishes and congregations. Deprived of their institutional "power," they got a new "glory" of a free, spontaneous, meaningful community. Their institutional element became important: it was a base— in many respects the only base—for Christian organization and service.

Not all congregations and parishes were capable of realizing this possibility. Some were nearly overwhelmed by the sociological changes in their own environment. Traditional patterns and contexts of service in their habitual environment collapsed, and many found it very difficult to seek and find new possibilities outside those patterns and contexts. This happened especially in the country, where the traditional way of life changed radically because of the upheavals of collectivization. Most of our congregations, however, discovered and grasped a new chance of becoming free communities of nonconforming Christian life. Contacts and encounters with those congregations became for many of us the source of the strongest inspiration for our work as theologians and Christians. I personally could hardly recall in all my ecumenical and ecclesiastical activities an experience which was of stronger encouragement to me than the regular contact with our congregations throughout the country in the fifties and sixties. I visited them Sunday by Sunday, speaking and listening. In all human perplexities, sometimes frustrations, the glory of Christian fellowship and mission kept emerging beyond any doubt.

No wonder that all through the years service in a local parish remained a meaningful vocation for our theologians in spite of the fact that from the financial point of view this was probably the least-paid occupation in the whole society. Hesitations with respect to that ministry, so strong and growing among theologians in other ecumenical situations, particularly in the United States, were expressed only occasionally.

Important as the parishes and the congregations proved to be, they were never the only form of Christian presence in the socialist society. They were a basis and a point of departure—not an end in themselves. A self-centered church is a "ghetto church," betrayal of all true biblical understanding of the church as a pilgrim church and as a "community of debtors." The presence of Christians cannot be only in expected places, in the organizations and institutions of Christian life. A living church always appears also in unexpected places (as her own Master,

Jesus of Nazareth, did—from the manger in Bethlehem to the cross on the Calvary). Here is one of the ecclesiological implications of a civilian interpretation.

In the climate of our Marxist society, this presence of the Christians in the unexpected places was difficult to achieve or maintain for an organized church. Christian possibilities of entering the secular realm were limited. The collapse of the Constantinian era narrowed the chances in this respect. The "automatic presence" of the church in public life (in feasts, festivals, public affairs, generally acknowledged rites) was eliminated. State administrations watched carefully that the church remained within its own institutional and religious precincts. For a church as institution it was not easy to transcend the boundaries toward her society. If she wanted to avoid the temptation of a self-centered ghetto church, she had to assert her presence in unexpected places in another way: through the presence of her own members and believers. It became very clear that individual Christian men and women, particularly laymen, were the real bearers of the apostolic witness in our socialist society. Men and women who worked as free and efficient citizens of their societies, who engaged in the fullness of their professional and human tasks, who at the same time lived as professing members of their congregations—they were the best examples of a civilian witness in action.

It is difficult to describe this Christian presence in unexpected places in general terms. There were no general patterns and blueprints for such a presence. It was sought for and discovered in the concrete situations of one's concrete life. Experiences shared and exchanged in the congregations helped very much in seeking and finding an orientation. And yet the decisive Christian witness often occurred in individual acts of obedience and love, in secular places, outside any immediate contact with a congregation. It occurred in the personal risk of word or act which in a given secular environment was easily misunderstood, opposed, even ridiculed, but which sometimes and with some people evoked a genuine curiosity, sympathy, and trust.

Let me recall some situations and examples of such a civilian witness in trying to introduce in a more concrete and personal way some of my friends and brethren as I remember them in their attempts to act as civilian Christians in some unexpected places of their life and work. The choice is arbitrary and incidental, but possibly exactly in that it might serve to introduce into, and to illuminate, the Christian presence in a socialist society.

WORKER   My friend František was originally a lawyer—and more than that. He was a high state official in the office of the President. Thus he had worked for years in close personal cooperation with Presidents Masaryk and Beneš. In the atmosphere after 1948 this was already sufficient to make him a potential enemy and suspect, although he was involved in no illegal or contrarevolutionary activities. Nevertheless, he was put before a trial and sentenced. After being released, there was no place for him in his original profession, and he had to become a worker. Such situations were not unusual in the fifties. Hundreds of thousands of people lost their original occupations and had to seek for a new profession. In some cases this was very bitter. For many people a profession is not just a way to earn money. Because they choose a job and practice it as a vocation, a breach in employment causes a crisis of identity and as such is a real human loss.

How should a Christian react in such a case? František avoided all dramatization of that situation. It was not easy for him, as a mature man and the father of a family, to learn a new profession—manual work demanding physical strength and ability. But he knew that there is a deeper level of personal identity. It is not just an identity of profession; rather it is an identity of confession. The backbone of personal life is faithfulness to one's own values and truths. Thus a forced change of profession might be a blow to one's personal plans and projects, yet it is not an "apocalyptic" blow. The way of a Christian man may be narrowed down, yet it remains open.

František tried to walk on that new, more difficult, and yet open way. The whole style of his life changed. His environment was quite different. He was a worker among the workers, handicapped at the outset by his lack of physical experience and know-how. Nevertheless, he moved ahead and did his new work well and intelligently. It was not easy to win the confidence of his fellow workers, especially since he was a clearly committed Christian. At first, he was a double outsider—a lawyer and a Christian. And yet his solidarity with the workers and his civilian witness of a faithful proexistence quickly made him a respected and trusted insider.

A striking proof of that occurred in 1968. One of the significant slogans and honest possibilities of the Czechoslovak spring of 1968 was the society's will to carry out an honest rehabilitation of all who had suffered injustice in the previous years. Thousands of people were rehabilitated. František was a clear case. The way back to some government office was opened. I asked him about it during one encounter in those days. I shall never forget the answer. "I do not seek any rehabilitation of this type. I have something more important to do now." And I learned what was more important: he was elected by his fellow workers to become a chairman of their important workers' union. He was right, for in terms of effective service to the welfare of his fellowmen this was a more important service. For me it was still more than that. His decision was a sign of civilian Christian witness exactly where the traditional debt of the churches was very deep: in effective solidarity with working people; an example of a genuine Christian witness in unexpected places.

PHYSICIAN   In some occupations the service of Christians became difficult in the fifties. Their very presence there was questioned. This applied, for instance, to teachers. Christian teachers were considered not to be sufficiently enlightened. But some other professions also became tenuous. One of these was the medical profession. Certainly, there was no ban on Christian doctors. They were not assigned to other activities, as were some lawyers. They were needed and respected. The problem generally arose when they were in higher positions as directors of hospitals or medical institutions.

I shall always remember a discussion with one of our very able physicians. As head of an important hospital department, he did great service to hundreds of patients. But he was given an ultimatum by his superiors: either he could end his active cooperation in the local congregation or he could give up his department. A leading and popular scientist and physician should not be a well-known practicing Christian. His decision was difficult. The doctor loved both his congregation and his hospital. How was he to decide? Would not the giving up of his responsible position in the hospital be irresponsible in terms of the welfare of those hundreds of patients? Would not relinquishing such a duty mean giving up important possibilities of a civilian witness, even if his active participation in the Christian life would have to cease—at least for some years? The physician weighed the possibilities and withdrew from the congregation. Many were distressed by his decision. Yet who would dare to be a self-righteous judge of this frustrating choice?

Another physician, my friend Jiří, took a different decision. He chose to remain an outspoken Christian and a member of his congregation. He was a genuine center of activities, especially in a very active group of younger couples, whom—among many others—he served as a devoted pediatrician. He was a young man—but with the best qualifications for an academic career. He was perfectly aware that he endangered his career by this "stubbornness."

And the situation sharpened. He was a man of clear professional ability and at the time a man of political integrity and open-mindedness toward the socialist system. So he was asked to join the Party. Generally, this was considered a gesture of honor and the opening for further academic possibilities. Jiří refused. He gave his clear reasons: his Christian convictions were incompatible with Marxism-Leninism. This was a risky refusal. Would it not be considered as an affront? Many people in similar situations preferred to accept—though without conviction, rather, on the contrary, against their own convictions. Yet Jiří's honesty was convincing: his act of confession did not make his situation more difficult. On the contrary, it won him respect and trust—not only among individuals but also within the Party. And there was no doubt about it: acts of personal honesty—though difficult in the atmosphere of pressures—were eventually the only creative acts and a service even for those who did not appreciate them. Here was a contribution of

Christians toward a democratization of our society, already in the years of Stalinism and in the later Novotný era.

ARTIST   Miroslav was a painter. And a very active presbyter in one of our experimenting congregations. He was deeply committed to his art and deeply committed to his church. This was not easy for him—neither in the artistic community nor in the church. He grew up as an artist in the period of "socialist realism." One way of artistic expression and one aspect of life were strongly recommended. Miroslav, as many young artists, did not want to move according to the suggested lines. His vision of life was different from the one-dimensional constructions of the official pattern. As a painter of the cross, he was clearly aware of the ambiguity and alienation of human life. And his way of expression was not descriptive realism; rather, he tried to discover the hidden method of abstract painting. He has not had much chance to be officially recognized under these circumstances, and he had practically no chance to sell his monumental paintings, for the individuals could hardly afford to buy them and the official galleries did not dare. Yet, as many other young artists, Miroslav did not compromise. He did not quit his "narrow way."

This way was not easy in the church either. There was a certain climate of distrust against a painting Christian in some of our congregations (a remnant of a Puritan-Calvinist mentality). And the emergency situation of the church seemed to discourage the luxury of artistic preoccupation. At the same time, Miroslav's style of painting did not encourage the understanding of church people. In his first period he portrayed the rugged Jesus of Nazareth and the raw reality of the world into which he entered, which challenged the conventional pious notions. And later his abstract method was evidently beyond the understanding of the majority of common people in our congregation.

Yet exactly in this way the value of honest civilian interpretation of the gospel became evident. Miroslav—and a whole group of our painters and artists—helped very much to counterattack a tendency toward a self-concerned ghetto church. Exactly in the emergency situation of a church, art is not a luxury; it guards the concern of the church to break through any pious ghetto and to be concerned about Christ's presence in the rugged world around us. Thus real art is vital for a vital church—particularly a contemporary art trying in its often new and irritating forms to illuminate the world as it really experiences it. And in the artistic community such a Christian art also bears its witness of faith testifying to the relevance of the cross for modern men and our alienated world.

Miroslav and his friends fulfilled this important function. It was good to see that their witness was not a cry in the desert. It was a sign of the vitality of the church that, overcoming its traditional and original distrust, it eventually accepted and supported its artists. Ecumenical contacts were important also in this respect; through them the artistic civilian interpretation was also able to speak abroad.

SCIENTIST   What can the world of science have in common with the world of religion? In our society the official ideological answer was emphatically clear: nothing whatever. Science and religion—this is light and darkness. Christians had to challenge this belief—all of them, in their everyday thought and orientation. In a specific way, this was the existential problem and the existential task of Christian scientists. They worked, understandably enough, in all the fields of science. In some, their presence was more difficult, that is, in those in which the ideological control (which, from a genuine scientific point of view, was often questionable) was stricter. This situation led many young Christians (who had to face some difficulties in being accepted in the universities) to choose mathematics and theoretical science as their profession. But even in the humanistic studies Christians went on working and made their distinctive contribution.

One example, in my opinion typical, involved the important research of two young Christian psychologists and their application to a very concrete need in our society. One of the results of the socialist revolution was a very general and generous network of kindergartens, nurseries, and institutions for babies. This was an achievement of socialist society. Infant mortality was radically reduced, and medical and social care was provided for all children without any cost to parents. This led some parents to rely on these institutions. Also, within the official climate of the society there was a trend emphasizing the importance of socialist institutions for little children and deemphasizing the importance of individual maternal and parental care. Our psychologists did not question the importance of effective institutions for socialist child care. But they discovered that the best collective care cannot fully compensate for the care of a personal and irreplaceable human mother. The analysis of psychological deprivation clearly led them to this solution.

It was not easy to assert these findings against the official trend of society. And it was not easy to affect the conscience and consciousness of the parents. Our psychologists did not give up. They got very effective help from film workers and television. Their film about the motherless children of our society had a great impact. The emphasis in our institutions changed. It became less ideological and more concretely human—certainly not to the detriment of socialist society.

Certainly, any scientist with good methods of research and a gift of observation and imagination might have been able to observe the phenomena and draw conclusions. And yet, in my opinion, it is perhaps not simply a chance that Christian psychologists were made attentive to this aspect of the human situation. The unconditional humanism of the gospel sharpened their eyes. And their imagination and perseverance was certainly a piece of a civilian witness to that unconditional humanism!

THEOLOGIAN   The coming of the socialist society has not meant any shortage in the number of theological students for our Protestant churches (in the Catholic Church the situation is much more difficult). The first years brought an outspoken boom; the number of theological students exceeded by far the needs of the churches. In the later fifties, the numbers dropped considerably and we started to worry. Yet the sixties brought again a continuing growth in applications. This was gratifying for our churches: young men and women entering study for the ministry chose a profession which did not promise any career from an economic or social point of view. Their decision for theology was costly.

In some situations, it was costly also with respect to the difficulties which had to be overcome. In the later fifties and early sixties, it was not easy to get into theological school straight out of high school. Some of the schools considered it a personal and institutional defeat if their graduates decided for theology. They tried to discourage them by different means of pressure. If the young students did not give up, eventually (even if sometimes with one or two years of delay) they succeeded. But sometimes they had to display a remarkable steadfastness and courage. In doing this, they sometimes won a genuine respect also among those who tried to bar their acceptance. I shall never forget the words of one official who tried to prevent one of the students from studying at the Comenius Faculty (he even ordered a psychiatric examination of the student and used other means of persuasion and pressure). However, after all this had proved to be in vain, he said as his last word: "If you had given up, we all would have lost much." Thus commitment to theology eventually won the respect of many opponents.

Such genuine existential commitment made theology attractive to many in the younger generation of the sixties, not only to those within the churches. Increasingly, candidates came as genuine (and very unconventional) converts without any ecclesiastical background in their families or personal history. Their style was different. In their appearance and way of life some of them scared many traditional churchmen. Yet at the same time they brought with themselves an element of radical honesty and evangelistic concern (though not in the traditional sense) for those outside our churches, for people in unexpected places on the margin of society.

Svatopluk was the best example of such a student. He was a trained vintner, a conscientious objector, as a result of that for some time a miner, a popular singer, a poet— and an evangelist. For some he was somehow suspect, a friend of publicans and sinners. He was not a brilliant student of theory. And yet he was a man of great honesty and passionate concern for human souls. I realized his gifts once in the mountains—in an unexpected place. The theological students who were spending a period of ski recreation there went into a pub for the evening. Many groups of young people were there. In this not very inspiring environment, Svatopluk was asked to sing his songs. He did, one after another—his own and other popular songs. The whole pub group eventually gathered together around him. And then he sang his spiritual songs. It was a clear witness to the human glory of God's Word. I never saw the light of the Sermon on the Mount so bright and helpful as in that pub in the mountains. And many of those who heard his song probably for the first time in their lives were very quiet and very concerned. A civilian witness in an unexpected place.

RENEWING THE CREDIBILITY
OF THE CHRISTIAN WITNESS

Our theological reflections about, and our practical examples of a civilian witness outlined a pattern of Christian witness for a post-Constantinian society. It is a *narrow way*. For the greater part of their existence in socialist society, Christian churches have been churches of rather limited possibilities. They have lost not only their privileges but also some of their legitimate chances and means. This has been painful, and it is not to be overlooked or even "glorified." The church as an institution has lost much of its significance for the public life of society. Opportunities for a direct, organized claim on society have become few and isolated. In this sense too the church—compared with its possibilities in an unbroken Constantinian order—has become poor. Therefore, the way is *narrow*.

And yet, at the same time our reflections and examples were able to point out that this way remains *open*. And it does not remain without promise. Amid all the unconcealed losses some new chances and possibilities emerged. The most meaningful one could be characterized as the *chance of a new credibility* of Christian existence in our society.

It cannot be denied that the credibility of the Christian church in the world today—in East and West alike—has been largely undermined. The history of modern secularization is also the history of the shrinking credibility of Christianity. And Constantinian Christianity is not without blame. The interpenetration of ecclesiastical institutions with the institutions of the society of the day, which was particularly obvious in the various forms of the union of "throne and altar," provided an opportunity to exert not only a dominating influence but also an unevangelical capitulation—and this unfortunately even more so. How often did the Constantinian church stand in its own way—fettered by false considerations of its own interests as an institution of the given order! And so the gospel was frequently hidden under a bushel— hidden from those very people who, travailing under a heavy social load, had been waiting for the justice of the Kingdom of God by word and deed. Thus, despite some outstanding achievements of a Christianly inspired philanthropy, the church and its message lost much of its credibility, especially through its failure to meet the social needs of modern industrial society. How many then arrived at the bitter conclusion: The church speaks of God—but it means its privileges and those of its society. It is a community of conscious or unconscious hypocrites.

The burden of this failure lies on us all. Yet now that the Constantinian opportunities have been lost we may be offered a new chance. It may be that a church which has no longer any privileges, and therefore no longer needs to defend itself, need no longer stand in its own way or in that of others, for in the post-Constantinian society the Christian can hardly be an opportunist. The one ground for becoming and remaining a Christian in that situation is the ground of faith. You have nothing to gain by being a Christian. Rather you may lose. Thus the shadow of hypocrisy grows less. And here is the chance for a new credibility. The mere existence of the Christian church can then already be a true witness. A community of pilgrims, of civilian men who do not seek to preserve any social privileges or to maintain any political "anticonceptions," who consciously live in the new society and take it seriously but who try to do so unequivocally as Christians—is not this presence of the Christian community within the Marxist-socialist world already a basic witness to society?

There were situations in which the reality of this new chance became visible in some of the most distinctive forms of the churches' activity, for example, immediately in their *preaching*. It is a real event to preach in our congregations. Some of us have had an opportunity to preach from many distinguished pulpits abroad. We considered this as a precious ecumenical gift. Yet most of us would hardly trade any of these noted pulpits for the modest pulpits in our congregations. For in our congregations an evidently poor and powerless word gained remarkable power and the glory of an officially unsupported, vulnerable, yet spiritually convincing truth. This is certainly not the case everywhere. There are also in our country staggering congregations and staggering pastors. And yet, taken as a whole, it is meaningful to preach in our situation.

This is valid also with respect to the missionary witness of Christians in the everyday context of their lives. In our discussion of Christians in unexpected places, it became clear that this witness is by no means easy. Very often such Christians are surrounded by secularized people, even by atheists. They cannot rely on a matter-of-course benevolence. Nevertheless, in one sense this witness is also easier than before. The Christian is "conspicuous." He is a visible exception. He is "questionable"—in a genuine sense: he evokes questions, and this is not always agreeable. Most people do not like to be asked the most personal, most existential—that is, the religious—questions. "Religion is a private matter"; too direct questions in this area hurt our "intimacy." Yet for a committed Christian to be "questionable" means also a genuine missionary chance. If we are asked questions, we have to give answers—and we *may* give answers. This is our chance to speak up and to be heard again—a chance of a credible witness.

All this particularly involves our lay people. As we suggested already, they are the real apostolic existence today —men and women participating in active solidarity, in the endeavors of their socialist society and at the same time living without compromise their Christian faith. Yet this new chance of credibility does not apply to lay people exclusively. It involves also the *clergymen* and *theologians*. The clergy as a sociological group have become considerably poorer—in terms of both economy and social prestige. A minister or a priest is not a "dignitary" anymore. He has to struggle for his existence, especially if he has a family. Yet exactly in this situation he has achieved a new and authentic dignity. There is a visible change. In our public opinion and also in much Czech literature of the last century, the clergyman was suspected and depicted as a hypocrite. The situation is very much different today. The minister or the priest is taken much more seriously —even in the arts and literature. He is, of course, an unusual type. "Questionable," surprising. Yet as such he is trusted as a man of honest decision and honest profession. He is credible again.

THE CHURCH AND
THE RENEWAL OF SOCIETY

At certain times it seemed that the only possible action
left to the churches with regard to society was the faithful
presence of individual Christians in the "expected and
unexpected places." This was so because of the deep distrust of the revolutionary society toward the church and
because of the ideological and administrative rigidity of
the political system. I think especially of the Stalinist era.
There was nothing passive in this presence; the patience
and the loyalty of the Christian—loyalty to Jesus Christ
and loyalty to the people of our society—helped to shape

the spiritual basis for a new and fresh service. And when the rigidity lessened, melting away, Christians got a new chance to participate in the spiritual and social ferment of their country.

With unique intensity, this occurred in the remarkable year of 1968. In this crucial year of Czechoslovak socialist society, a new and creative program emerged out of deep crisis; it was the program of a radical democratization of a socialist society. Christians were not the initiators of this program. It was conceived and carried out primarily on initiative from the center of political power itself, the Communist Party under the new leadership of Alexander Dubček. Yet this Communist program immediately achieved a positive response from Christians. This did not spring out of opportunistic reasons; it was not because the new regime opened fresh possibilities for Christian churches. This was, of course, one of the important changes and achievements of the democratization.

Christian support of the new developments had deeper motivations. The idea of a "socialism with a human face" was very close to Christians' own hearts. The model of democratic socialism was not alien to them. An attempt to keep the basic structural changes of socialism and, at the same time, to respect the individual right of every socialist citizen corresponded to some of their own deepest insights and expectations. Certainly, democratic socialism is not simply the incarnation of the biblical vision. None of our "secular cities" is to be identified with the New Jerusalem. We remained soberly aware of the tentativeness and vulnerability of the new program. And yet, does not the prophetic call to justice and solidarity with the oppressed and underprivileged *and* the apostolic message of the inalienable right of every human person in Christ encourage the Christian to seek and to move in this direction? Thus many of us were fascinated by the new model of our "secular city."

Czechoslovak Protestants had still more specific reasons to welcome the process of renewal within their society. Did not this process clearly revive some of the deepest visions of our reformation? Did not the Hussite tradition emphasize exactly that dialectical unity of the demands both for revolutionary social justice and for the freedom of every human being in search for truth? Right in the center of Prague, the Jan Hus monument represents this legacy of the Czech reformation with its engraved message: "Love each other and let every one share in truth." It was not a matter of chance that exactly this place and this program became the rallying point and the inspiration for renewal in our society. Its program was evidently more than a short-lived political experiment. The inspiration for a democratic socialism came out of the depth of our most creative spiritual heritage. No person was so much present and alive in the Prague spring of 1968 as Jan Hus and his legacy.

The process of democratization opened new possibilities for Christian participation in our society. For the first time, Christians were unambiguously recognized as fully qualified and responsible members of their society. They were respected not only as citizens in spite of their Christianity but as Christians who were citizens of their own specific faith and confession, of their own specific contribution to their society. One's being a "religious man" ceased to be a minus point for a Christian active in his profession and his society. Consequently, Christians were not simply tolerated; they were expected to contribute in their own distinctive way and perspective to the formulation and realization of our common social goals. Theological faculties and students participated with great intensity in the thought and action of the academic community. Pastors and laymen were active on all levels of public life. I was the first Christian after nearly two decades who was invited repeatedly to speak on Czechoslovak radio as a Christian. For the first time, public meetings of Christians and Marxists were organized not only in the universities and the churches but in the biggest halls of our cities. The first of such public dialogues, in April, 1968, in Prague, attracted more than 3,000 people for a five-hour session of intensive exchange, with passionate participation from people in the audience. Thus Christians started to play a new role in socialist society.

This situation brought with it a new test of the credibility of our existence as churchmen and theologians in our society. Many new possibilities for Christian churches opened. How were we to use them? There was a strong temptation on the Christian side to consider the new atmosphere as a sign of weakness of Marxist society and as the signal for a possible Christian counterattack and retaliation for all the limitations and difficulties imposed on the churches in the past. This temptation seemed to be natural; especially for the powerful churches who lost much—such as the Roman Catholic Church—it seemed to be the logical behavior. There was much to ask for. The "rehabilitation" (the great word and great spirit of our society in 1968) had to include also the churches, for example, the Roman Catholic religious orders, which were severely afflicted after 1948. The decisive question was: Will the churches ask only for a legitimate rehabilitation in such cases of clear injustice and for fairer possibilities enabling a more effective service in their society or will they push further toward recapturing some lost privileges of the past? Will they be concerned more about themselves or about the people whom they should serve, the people of their society?

I speak about a "test case of Christian credibility" in this connection, because the new possibilities immediately raised the question: Is our theological and spiritual struggle for a new credible way as a post-Constantinian church a genuinely new orientation? Are our slogans of a "servant church," "community of pilgrims," and "congregation of debtors" simply emergency slogans enforced on us by our changed situation? Will they be forgotten the moment the situation changes again? Will we rush back to the old good days of Constantinian privileges?

This temptation was not so strong for the minority groups of Protestants. It was much stronger for the more powerful (and in the past also more restricted) Roman Catholic Church. However, because the future of Christian churches in a secularized world will evidently be the common one, the ecumenical one, we looked with expectations to our bigger sister, the Roman Catholic Church. We were grateful that it basically overcame this temptation. Catholic bishops (some of them after years of exemplary Christian conduct in profane occupations!) responded to the new situation in the spirit of a servant church. The influence of the Vatican Council, though somehow delayed and not as effective in our Catholicism as abroad, still considerably helped the Roman Catholic Church to find a responsible orientation in the new situation.

Thus theological attempts at a new orientation of Christian churches in the post-Constantinian age, undertaken in the difficult situation of limitations and pressures, were probably not in vain. The churches found their place and their open way in the new society. They became the churches of a socialist society. The *churches,* not simply the fellow travelers of the leading ideology. But the churches of their *society,* in critical solidarity with its efforts. In the hour of its own opening, society recognized this role of its churches.

One of the most moving symbols of the new place of the church in its society and at the same time of the new solidarity between the church and society was the curious symphony of all the church bells with all the factory sirens in August, 1968, as a unanimous—though also "disharmonious"—confession of support for the program of democratic socialism. The realization of this program became much more difficult after intervention from the outside in August, 1968. Yet the experience of the new loyalty and solidarity between the church and state remains. It was an important symbolic act in the fall of 1968 when the President of the socialist republic, Ludvik Svoboda, expressed—for the first time after decades—the appreciation and gratitude of the highest representative of the state to all the churches for their stand in the spring and in August. How were we to evaluate this gesture? As a Constantinian scene in the Prague Castle? By no means. No new privileges were awarded; no protective guarantees were given for the churches on their further way—which became much more uncertain again. But possibly this was a symbol of open possibilities for a meaningful service of the Christian church in a socialist society.

THEOLOGY
IN DIALOGUE

THEOLOGY
AND REVOLUTIONARY CHANGE

What is the place of theology in times of revolutionary change? What is its role in a church which has to struggle not only for its more meaningful mission but for its sheer survival? Is there any place at all for theology in such circumstances? Or does such a situation provide the final proof (which might have been suspected as fact by many in the church already in more normal times and situations) that theology is only a delayed and cooled-down rationalization of spiritual insights and historical events? Isn't theology a "late bird," like her sister philosophy, the "owl of Minerva (according to Hegel), starting her flight only in the "evening after?" Isn't she then necessarily more an obstacle than a help in a situation of radical challenge? Should not then theology really be the first sack of sand which, on a stormy sea, the true disciple should throw overboard to be able to save the ship for a new mission on the other side of the raging storm?

Many persons in ecumenical theology today argue in this fashion. I often heard such voices among younger theologians in the United States. Action, not reflection, is the proof of a Christian in a revolutionary age. Theology does not seem to be much good for an engaged Christian today.

Theology is not without guilt in this situation of contempt and disregard. There is indeed a type of theology which is of little help in a situation of radical challenge. Churches in Czechoslovakia became clearly aware of this in facing the collapse of the Constantinian order. How much of the traditional theology of the church appeared clearly Constantinian! If the Constantinian era was characterized by the alliance between pope and emperor then there is no doubt about it: The spirit of that fusion characterized also much of Christian theology—in its form, in its approach, in its social perspective. In its *form,* in that peculiar alliance between Athens and Jerusalem, in which much of the dynamic biblical message got caught up in the metaphysical structures of Greek and Roman thought. (Much of the unrest in theology today, including the "death of God theology," might then be understood as a reaction to the Constantinian thought form!) In its *approach,* how often theology (and theologians) participated in the arrogance of the Constantinian church in approaching the world as patronizing *patres et magistri,* fathers and teachers, presenting their infallible answers in the spirit of self-centered dogma and monologue! In its *social perspective,* how often theology provided the ideological justification for the establishment, emphasizing nearly exclusively its concern for the "law and order" of the status quo! Such a theology doesn't help much. Indeed, it is a late bird, at its best a Sleeping Beauty, at its worst the opiate of the people. It is utterly legitimate and understandable for a concerned Christian (as it was legitimate for a concerned atheist) to turn his back on such a theology.

Yet this turning of the back would be misunderstanding and confusion within a Christian church if it were generalized and absolutized against theology as such. Like the church itself, theology cannot be identified with its Constantinian type. There is also the theology of the biblical prophets and apostles, an intellectual network of the fishermen. This is a different theology. In its *form,* it is a biblical theology, the thought of the exodus, concerned about God's commitment to man in history, trying in thought and action to interpret this commitment into the perplexities of history and society today. In its *approach,* it is a theology of dialogue—the dialectical thought of pilgrims who do not claim ready-made dogmas and blueprints but who think and live as Socratic evangelists, in honest give and take with their fellow pilgrims. In its *social perspective,* it is a theology of the Kingdom and of its righteousness, challenging all the justice and injustice of human laws and orders and opening the possibilities for creative change.

Such a theology—a theology of the exodus, of dialogue, and of change—is not an obstacle but a decisive help to a church in a revolutionary situation. It does not water down the action. Its heart is not an idea but the event of salvation and liberation; its fundamental element is not detached reflection but obedience. But on the other hand it does not absolutize the action—it is concerned about the light for the action, in the vision of faith, and in human analysis. Thus it helps to keep the action a truly human action, an articulated step, a step toward a human end, a move of humanization. This task of articulation is also a concern and a genuine contribution of the Christian church in society. A church of pilgrims is not just a church of nomads. It is not a movement of blind enthusiasts. It is the church of the Word, and as such the church of vision and thought. In this sense, theology is an inalienable function of the church—in the days of stability *and* in the days of revolution.

The existence and experience of our churches in socialist society was a very vivid proof of the vital importance of theology in revolutionary change. The charisma of Czech Protestantism contained and brought about strong presuppositions for developing a non-Constantinian type of theology. Openings for a theology of exodus, of dialogue, and of revolution were deeply rooted in the heritage of the Czech reformation. And the developments in that theology in the last generation helped to evolve and to display those presuppositions. Let us list some examples of those helpful possibilities:

1. The work of J. L. Hromádka between the two wars, both in his concentration on the prophetic and apostolic message and in his widely open social and cultural orientation with a great passion for history and social change.

2. The intensive biblical theology of S. Daněk and especially of J. B. Souček, a theologian of a "circumspective faith" and exceptional theological erudition; during World War II, he organized in semi-illegal courses (universities were closed for Czechs by the Germans) excellent theological training for a strong group of young

theologians who later proved to be well-prepared theological and ecumenical leaders of their church in coming decades.

3. A broad basis of theologically interested laymen in the congregations, who had emerged especially from the youth groups during the war.

4. The amazing publishing activity of the Hus and Comenius Faculties (under a very bold editorial policy of librarian V. Sobotka). All this created presuppositions for creative and extensive theological work. Thus the radical change of 1948 did not catch our theologians unprepared.

The center of theological studies of Czech Protestants in the fifties and sixties was without any doubt the Comenius Faculty in Prague (founded in 1950 as heir to the old Hus Faculty, the first modern theological faculty of Czech Protestants founded in 1918). It was not the only theological school in Czechoslovakia. There was a Lutheran Faculty in Bratislava (Slovakia), a school of distinguished tradition. There was the new Hus Faculty of the Czechoslovak Church in Prague, which played an important role in its own church and was a living proof of the importance of theological work for a church in a search of a new biblical orientation. There was Eastern Orthodox Faculty in Prešov (Slovakia). There were two strong Catholic faculties, but they were considerably handicapped by the difficulties both within the church and from the outside.

The presence of these theological schools in our post-Constantinian situation was a providential chance. Czech Protestants felt this to be especially true with regard to the Comenius Faculty, which was probably the best-known theological school both within its own society and in the ecumenical world. Why was this presence so important?

We suggested already some general reasons for the importance of theological work for church and society. In a Marxist society there was one additional reason for this. This society was not an ideologically neutral system. It was ideologically oriented. This, as such, did not necessarily mean that the church also should have become more than ever an ideological—that is, a dogmatically minded —church. In a "dogmatic society" the church should be, by its very existence, a champion of intellectual freedom and open-mindedness. Her contribution to the climate of society is rather an emphasis on the transideological dimension both of the Christian message and of man in his nature and history.

"Transideological emphasis," however, does not mean disregard of ideology. On the contrary, intellectual ambiguity or amorphousness is never a quality of the true church—particularly not when it is facing an ideologically concerned environment. If the church really wants to become a church of its society, it has to take its ideological orientation seriously. If the church wants to open a real contact with society, it has to respond to society's program and underlying philosophy. It has to give an articulate response to an articulate challenge. Otherwise it would be just a pious ghetto, not what a church really should be: the partner in a possible dialogue. Thus a church concerned about its dialogical place in society has necessarily to be a theologically minded church. In this sense it became very clear indeed that theology is substantially more than a luxury or ornament for easy days; it is the fundamental presupposition for the responsible orientation of a church in a revolutionary society.

The four following sections touch on some crucial problems of our theological orientation in a Marxist society. They do not pretend to cover the whole range of the problems with which we were confronted, in a systematic or even balanced way. They rather pick up the questions with which I personally dealt in my theological work. I did so not for myself only—not just out of private and capricious choice—but as a theologian of my church, participating in search of a responsible orientation in a socialist society.

In this connection—as acts and stages of a theology in dialogue—the following issues emerged as particularly important:

The problem of secularization: a Marxist society poses with unique urgency the challenge of a radically secularized society. How is one to respond to this challenge? Is secularization for the Christian church a calamity or a chance for a new beginning? Is confession of Christian faith—the confession that Christ is Lord—honestly possible in a secularized world?

The problem of ideology: a particular edge in the challenge of Marxist society to church and theology is given with the fact that it is an ideologically founded and ideologically minded society. How is one to evaluate this sharp and pretentious claim? What is a responsible relation between theology and ideology?

The problem of atheism: the ideology of a Marxist society is clearly atheist. This creates in many respects a new situation for Christians in that environment. The most articulate ideological representatives in such a society are atheists. How is one to approach them, and how can one deal theologically with the problem of atheism?

The task and the gift of dialogue: in all our deliberations about the mission of the church in a Marxist society the theme of dialogue emerged as our major theological concern. For years it seemed only a very distant and somehow nebulous *task*. It was to be taken seriously even then—in the spirit of "hope against hope" that dialogue with the Marxist would be possible—one day. It was to be taken seriously in search for a theological orientation which would help to eliminate the obstacles and barriers on our way to that future. A positive, unbiased approach to such problems as secularization, ideology, and atheism is to be understood in this context.

The task became a *gift*. The hope did not disappoint; dialogue became possible and developed in Czechoslovakia with exceptional intensity. It created a phenomenon in which Czechoslovak theologians and Czechoslovak Marxists were able to present a distinctive contribution not only to their own society (especially with respect to the democratization of socialist society) but even in a broader ecumenical and cultural context. Thus a report about the dialogue logically constitutes the concluding chapter of the section—and of the whole book on the church in a Marxist society.

JESUS CHRIST
IN A SECULARIZED WORLD

A PARALYZING PARADOX?　　The Christian church opened its historical mission with the proclamation of its faith in the ultimate commitment of God to man in Jesus Christ. *Kyrios Christos*—Christ is the Lord: this was the most concise and probably the most original confession of Christian faith. All through its history, the church kept this confession, though not always with the same concentration and emphasis. There were periods and trends in which general ideas about God or general ideas about man weakened Christological concentration. And yet again and again, the specific Christological core of Christian theology and anthropology broke through all Christian teaching and preaching.

With special intensity this seems to be the case in churches today. The theme of the Lordship of Christ is the focal point of ecumenical interest. Bibliographies of theological works of recent decades, ecumenical study projects, programs of ecclesiastical conferences, and consultations evidence this vividly: such key words as the "Kingship," the "Lordship," and the "finality" of Jesus Christ appear with amazing frequency.

This fact is not a matter of course. Indeed, it may be anything but a matter of course to a sober observer. For if one confronts this ecumenical accentuation with the historical-phenomenological situation of the church in the second half of the twentieth century, one can hardly escape the impression of a peculiar paradox. It is especially felt when one exposes oneself to the perspective of outsiders (and the church, in its own interest, should also expose itself to such a perspective attentively and open-mindedly!), for example to the analyses of Marxist historians and philosophers. Is there not a tremendous contradiction there?

This could well have been different in the past. In certain historical epochs and conditions such a message appeared quite justified and understandable, for example in the ancient Orient and in Hellenistic classical antiquity. The confession "Yahweh is King" and "Jesus Christ is Lord" was, to be sure, provocative but understandable, in view of the very ancient, and at the time almost generally predominant, ontocracy (conception of the world as an unchangeable chain of sacred being) with its sacral kingdom as the apex of the cosmic-social structure.

And this accentuation was perhaps also understandable

in the Christian Middle Ages, when the claim of Jesus Christ to be king also found, in a very real sense, a social analogy (whether the analogy was a genuine one or not is another question). Theocratic structures—in the Orthodox Byzantinian form of Caesaropapism or in the equally effective, politically and socially, Roman form of an ecclesiocracy—determined the political spirit of the times as well as political reality. Particularly within the Constantinian model of a *corpus Christianum,* Christian civilization, the witness to the Lordship of Christ seemed to be plausible, in accordance with the social, or at least cultural, predominance of Christianity.

But today? Has not our world become radically different precisely in this regard? One need only think of that thought form in the background of which the idea of the Kingship and Lordship of Yahweh and Jesus Christ took its form. Oriental ontocracy and that of classical antiquity has been shaken to its very depth—to be replaced by technocracy. Our world is no longer predetermined in a sacral-ontological sense. Our world has been demythologized and left to us for responsible technical mastery. The old mythological-metaphysical structures of thought no longer appeal to modern man—and most certainly not the idea of a sacral lordship related to these structures. Political life is moving—despite all the setbacks still possible— from theocratic to democratic structures; it is becoming more and more unequivocally secularized.

Secularization in fact is becoming one of the typical signatures of our time. The phenomena are known and generally visible: progressive secularization and alienation from the church of almost all areas of social life (economics, politics, science, the arts, morality, and philosophy) and the retreat of religion to "ultimate questions," indeed the fact that for many the religious question as such has fallen silent—therefore the "silence of God," that phenomenon of modern life which is described by modern art with such frankness. It is true for most people that they live as though God did not exist (*etsi Deus non daretur*)—and they do so either with the euphoria of those who have finally come of age or with the cool objectivity and technology of the skeptical generation. In any case, the "Lordship of Jesus Christ" is an idea which can scarcely be imagined or realized in this world. The feeling that it belongs to an alien world —which may also hold good for other aspects of the biblical message—is decidedly true for the man of this secularized world who has come of age and is weary of authority, precisely in the face of this claim and this doctrine. If then the church refers to, and bases its message on, the Lordship of Christ with particular concentration, it seems only to be reaching into emptiness.

The paradox of this situation is almost universal in the church throughout the world. But it concerns the churches of Eastern Europe with particular sharpness, especially perhaps those of our churches which grew out of the Bohemian reformation. On the one hand, the message of the Lordship of Jesus Christ has been preserved with particular intensity in the heritage of this reformation. As we have already pointed out in our short historical orientation, this stress was almost constitutive for it. Already for the Hussites, the royal authority of Jesus Christ, the undivided claim of this sovereign Lord to all areas of life, became the real driving force of their revolutionary attempts to reform the church—and society! And it also holds true for the Bohemian Brethren, "these silent ones in the land," with their "theocracy of love" (F. M. Dobiaš), that is, with their untiring endeavor to take seriously, in all areas and relationships of life, the "law of Jesus Christ" as grace and a call to disciple-ship. No wonder Comenius felt a particular obligation, in his *Testament of the Unity of the Brethren,* to admonish his brethren to take care "to wish Christ to be among you in the future not only as prophet of pulpit, not only as priest and bishop of the altar, but as king of the throne and of the scepter to exercise judgment over the disobedient." This testament was never silenced by the Czech evangelical church, and it has prevailed until today as a particular stress in the thinking of this church. Thus the general emphasis on the Lordship of Christ in the church throughout the world has a particular sharpness among us.

On the other hand, there is in our situation a particular edge also to that phenomenon which in the context of the modern world seems to make problematic the emphasis on the Lordship of Christ. I refer to secularization. For, in our country, this is not simply a general process, as occurs in all other technologically developed countries; it is also programmatically fostered. All official strata of social life are to be structured on the basis of an ideology which is radically critical of religion and church. Thus the idea of a *corpus Christianum* is superseded, as a social model, by the model of a programmatically secularized society. If one faces this situation with all its consequences clearly and soberly, one must ask: Where is there a socially effective and therefore credible verification of a claimed and proclaimed Lordship of Christ? Truly, the paradox of such a proclamation in such a society is tremendous.

Here we face one of the crucial problems of a theological orientation in a Marxist society: What does it mean when the church attempts to testify, or pretends to testify, to the Lordship of Christ with particular emphasis in the radically secularized world of today? Is it succumbing to the spirit of a self-deceiving or deceptive utopia in which reality is by-passed in the fashion of the enthusiasts? Or is it succumbing to a spiritual schizophrenia which behaves the more radically in its claims the more helpless it becomes in actuality? Or, in this attitude of the church, do we have to do with a flight forward through the front line because all attempts to cover a retreat in the face of a general alienation from the church have been tried and have been to no avail? All this could be possible. But all these attitudes would be doomed to failure. For one cannot, in the long run, build a church upon fictions. Is there, on the other hand, an honest and credible solution to this paradox—credible especially in view of our secularized fellowmen within and outside the church?

One can, of course, reject such questions as pseudoquestions and ignore this paradox; for example, in a fundamentalistic-pietistic manner in which one simply finds radical changes in our secularized world to be an apostasy, and thus withdraws into the center of security of faith in order to dispense with concrete analyses of the modern situation. Many people—not only individuals but also congregations, especially in Eastern Europe, for example—give their true testimony in the complete paradox of their pious existence in a world imprinted by atheism. Nevertheless one cannot regard this way as one which is generally satisfactory, especially with regard to the outsiders to whom we owe a credible proclamation. Part of this concern for credibility also necessitates thinking about how one can honestly face this paradox of the Lordship of Christ in a secularized world. What is the nature of this paradox? Is there in our theme not only an undeniable and serious tension between its two poles, the Lordship of Christ and the secularized world, but rather an exclusive and paralyzing contradiction? Does secularization simply exclude the Lordship of Christ—and vice versa? Have we only an either-or alternative and, consequently, have we to choose between dogmatic and authoritarian fundamentalism or secular and relativistic modernism?

SECULARIZATION—CALAMITY OR POSSIBILITY? For most of the secular analysts of secularization, there is only a positive answer to this question. Verifiable phenomena actually seem to favor this answer. What can be grasped statistically, what is brought to light by sociological and psychological research, what comparative philosophical and intellectual-historical reflections attempt to establish—all seem to point in this direction: the power and the radiation of the church is decreasing—and with it, to all appearances, the authority of its Lord, the authority of Jesus Christ.

Traditional thinking in the church also tends toward the same conclusion. Within its perspective, secularization largely appears as apostasy and calamity, as alienation and alienness. Accordingly, a more or less negative attitude toward the revolutionary changes of the secularized world prevailed for centuries—and, among the broadest layers of Christianity, it continues until today. This is "natural" in a certain sense. For it is quite clear that for the church this process is connected with losses, especially when it is a question not only of a general secularization and alienation from the church but also of a programmatic secularization and alienation—as in Eastern Europe. Then the reaction which suggests itself is just that—reaction, such as attempts apologetically to check, to resist, and, where possible, to counterattack this trend. The church has tried to assume this attitude again and again; the history of its encounters with the modern world (one need only recall ecclesiastical controversy with secularizing and secularized science) has been marked by it. Advancing secularization, the coming of age of modern man in economics, politics, and culture, was regarded overwhelmingly as a hostile front.

This attitude is, in my opinion, futile and (together with the reasoning behind it) false. To establish the first judgment is almost too easy, for the futility becomes visible in the results: the church's line of defense led to one defeat after another. No great wisdom is needed today to establish this. It is more important to realize that it was also theologically false, quite apart from pragmatic success or failure. Ecumenical theological work during the last decades has rendered a remarkable service in this respect, from the prophetic suggestions of Dietrich Bonhoeffer, via the analyses of Friedrich Gogarten, the sketches of a theology of history of Arend T. van Leeuwen, to the American theologians of the secular, such as Harvey Cox or Paul van Buren. I would like to stress three points in this connection—that is, in the attempt to attain a new, perhaps a theologically more appropriate orientation in the face of the problem of secularization, building upon the positive results of this ecumenical study.

1. In an undifferentiatedly negative attitude toward secularization, the fact that the church shares the responsibility for secularization is all too easily forgotten. One cannot overlook the fact (and many of the above-mentioned ecumenical voices seem to have established this emphatically) that the phenomenon of modern secularization can hardly be conceived apart from its biblical background. Naturally this process was also determined by other historical components, and one should not over-

simplify it. A constellation of the most varied factors and conditions was involved. But the church, in particular, made a decisive contribution to the process—not as an ecclesiocratic institution but as the bearer of the proclamation entrusted to it. For this proclamation of the creation and redemption of the world in Jesus Christ (and in our context one must add quite emphatically: the proclamation of his Lordship) also meant, in its consequences, a radical demythologization, a desacralization of the world. The world is not divine, it is created—it is creation. And it is the world saved and liberated by Christ; it is not a realm of blind forces of fate and of demons. This has consequences for basic human situations. In this world of liberated creation, man is not a servant or slave of natural or supernatural cosmic elements, not a slave of demonic powers, but rather the redeemed, liberated, and empowered son (Galatians 4:7). This proclamation and its corresponding faith opened up a completely new perspective to man with regard to the natural world; the way was opened to free and responsible knowledge and action.

2. In the negativistic attitude toward the process of secularization, the positive possibility of this process was very easily overlooked. Secularization originally meant secularization of ecclesiastical property. By this was meant at first simply the relinquishing of material property by the church as an institution. But could not one also use the term meaningfully in a figurative sense, as a designation for the secularization of the spiritual property of the church, of ecclesiastical "talents" and "gifts" —the unraveling of ecclesiastical accumulation for the world? This may happen very ambiguously—and it did happen very ambiguously in modern European history.

Nevertheless, one should not overlook the positive possibility: Does not this process also contain a missionary opportunity, in the true sense of the word *missio*: a distribution of the spiritual and intellectual goods entrusted to the church into areas which otherwise could hardly be reached by the institutional church? Was not, in the spirit of the gospel, a great service rendered in this way, accompanied by alienation of various kinds, but still sometimes with astonishing positive effect, perhaps in opposition to, and under the stubborn protests of, the part of the constituted church and established Christendom, but nevertheless corresponding in some measure to the gospel? Think, for example, of the humanist impulses which, on the basis of the biblical message, also helped to shape non-Christian movements. Should one not praise God, therefore, even though, from an ecclesiastical-patriotic viewpoint, the taste of such praise may seem bitter? When, for example, impulses of ecclesiastical philanthropy had to give way to generous, programmatic structures of the public system of health and education? Should one not assess positive things as positive, even though ecclesiastical philanthropic institutions are, under certain circumstances, secularized in the process? The church has never been commissioned to keep its talents exclusively as privileged property or as its own investment; on the contrary, it was commissioned to serve humanity, and thus to place its gifts at the disposal of the world as well.

3. But the negativist attitude toward secularization is particularly false because it threatens to overlook the fact that secularization could remind the church of the real concern of the gospel. Could not a true renunciation of ecclesiastical privileges, a giving up of the gifts of the church to the world, therefore correspond to the central movement of the gospel, the path of God to man, that is, the saving renunciation of the Son of God on behalf of

the world? In this connection one should take Philippians 2 very seriously. The path of God to man is explained and described there with the words, he "did not count equality with God a thing to be grasped, but emptied himself (giving up what was his), taking the form of a servant." Does this passage—or rather, this paradigm—not prescribe the way of a servant church, the church giving up what it has for the world? And does it not, in this sense, lay bare the true nucleus of a legitimate secularization? Could not the church, by refusing in this sense to have anything to do with secularization, in fear of losing its property (be it material or spiritual), actually be refusing to have anything to do with discipleship? Perhaps it would not be an exaggeration to state that what is at stake in the spiritual wrestling for a true understanding of secularization is, in the final analysis, also a true concept of the church—namely, whether the church moves within the movement of its Lord, upon the path of the serving congregation, or whether it builds its own, opposite, egocentric path. Therein lies one of the most portentous decisions of church history.

If I understand correctly, this concern was understood in the Czech reformation in an exemplary manner. The call to apostolic poverty was one of the basic ecclesiological accents of the Hussites as well as of the Bohemian Brethren. The Third Article of Prague states quite clearly "that secular power and property should be taken away from priests and monks, and all should be induced to lead the obedient life according to the apostolic model." After the classic Reformation demands of the free proclamation of the Word of God and of a proper celebration of the Lord's Supper, this third demand follows immediately in these words: apostolic discipleship—and secularization! This close connection may to some appear to be a sign of hazy enthusiasm (*Schwärmerei*). According to our understanding, there is here a deep realization (which was perhaps not as clearly given in the later Reformation) that what is indivisibly at stake in the reformation of the church is also a wrestling for evangelical obedience encompassing all of life; quite emphatically also a wrestling for the true form and movement of the church, and for a return to the apostolic church. When this is acknowledged, one can never reject secularization in principle as apostasy and calamity.

Precisely this third point is to be maintained in full measure even in the face of the programmatic overthrow of the Constantinian order. One cannot deny that in this change the church has to swallow much that is bitter. It loses much. This should be seen clearly, and it should not be glorified. The fall of ecclesiastical institutions is sometimes cheered from the theological gallery in the attempt at a positive evaluation of secularization. The phenomenon of the world come of age is often linked with an optimistic philosophy of history. I have no wish to join in that. "The secularized world is not the best of all possible worlds" (G. Bassarak). And to approach this from the other angle, the Constantinian church is not simply to be condemned; its possibilities are to be seen as such. But the decisive thing is that the gospel is not bound to these possibilities; this particular form that the history of the church has produced is not the only one. Indeed, it is truly not the preferable one, but rather a particularly vulnerable and dubious one. It is precisely in this alliance of the church with the secular order and power of the state that a sinister liaison of the bride of Christ with the bridegrooms of this world occurs very easily; this is where the temptation of any *corpus Christianum* lies.

Petr Chelčický expressed this in an unsurpassably vivid

manner at the height of the Hussite movement (in the midst of a still unbroken Constantinian age!). He regarded the Constantinian alliance as historical Christianity's fall into original sin. Let us recall once more his graphic imagery: two gigantic whales—the pope and the emperor—had torn the "net of faith." To such a viewpoint a radical secularization can appear not only as a calamity but also as an opportunity, the possibility to finally break with illegitimate relations, to reject the temptation of clericalism once and for all, and not simply to defy the shaking of the foundations of the Constantinian house. For when the church is thrown into the necessity of renunciation of any kind of grasping at things, it does not fall into a vacuum outside the Lordship of its Lord but, on the contrary, continues to live and to suffer —and perhaps now quite emphatically—under his imperishable promise. To shut oneself off from this possibility from the very beginning is spiritually the most dubious mark of any and every negativism toward secularization.

If we try to apply the results of our considerations to the question of the Lordship of Christ today, then hopefully it becomes clear that secularization in no way needs to mean only a dissolution of the Lordship of Christ. All three considerations have pointed in this direction:

1. if secularization is also conditioned by the gospel (expressed concretely, by the proclamation of the liberating Lordship of Christ over all powers);

2. if it includes the positive possibility to convey certain "goods," "talents," and "gifts" of the evangelical heritage in this world to a greater extent than the institutional church ever could;

3. if the church (wherever it has ears to hear and eyes

to see) is, in the fall of false alliances, reminded therein of its true form and is thrown into its constitutive, emptying, servant movement; then one cannot by any means regard it as a fatal revolutionary overthrowing of the Lordship of Christ.

And one can perhaps say even more. The images and the message of Philippians 2:5–11 shone out for us at a significant point in our reflections concerning the spiritually positive possibilities of secularization. But this text is simultaneously one of the basic passages of the evangelical proclamation of the Lordship of Christ! The path of the Son of God which led to the "emptying of himself" is the path of his Lordship. "Therefore God has highly exalted him and bestowed on him the name which is above every name." It pays to reflect on this. Is not light from this context thrown also upon our subject? The path of the church which has led into the alienness of the secular world—the paradox of our theological situation today—no longer, in the light of the path of the Son of God which led him into alienation, has to rob us of his presence. Rather, it can bring us nearer to him—in accord with the incomparable paradox of the path of his Lordship.

Here lies a spiritual chance for a church in a post-Constantinian society: to awake once more to the proper biblical vision and promise of the Lordship of Christ. On the ruins of the Constantinian structures the New Testament good news of Jesus Christ might be liberated from its theocratic captivity and thus be understood again in its authenticity as the good news of the Lord who is the servant—the servant who is the Lord. Then a new, modest, yet meaningful way opens for a more credible proclamation of the Lordship of Christ in a secularized society.

IDEOLOGY
AND TOLERANCE

One of the difficult tasks for a theology in a Marxist society was the theological problem of ideology. The distinctive characteristic of that society, as we just saw while dealing with the question of secularization, was its emphasis on ideology as the normative basis of all public life. How is one to respond to such a claim? What is the value and the function of ideology in society? What is its meaning in a theological perspective? And what are the practical implications for a dialogical coexistence between people of different creeds? What is the relation between ideology and tolerance?

It was not easy to find an unbiased theological approach to these questions. Ideological dogmatism in the fifties and still in the early sixties tempted us to retaliate in theological denunciations of ideology. And there was much negativism with regard to ideology in the prevailing trends of Continental theology. Yet a more open, critical, but differentiating theological reflection seemed to be necessary for a responsible orientation in a Marxist society. The following section tries to trace such a possibility.

Reflections respond to a climate of deep theological and cultural distrust toward ideology, as has been characteristic especially of German theology in the last decades. This climate is different from the American cultural scene. Yet the basic thesis, emphasizing theological responsibility for positive dialogical participation in constructive ideological work in our societies, seems to me no less valid in the American social and cultural context than in our society. Are not attempts at ideological clarification of emerging social issues one of the major needs of contemporary American society? In this sense, theological reflections on the problem of ideology might be of some interest also for American readers.

A RIFLEMEN'S FESTIVAL   "What we have nowadays could be called a riflemen's festival with ideology as the target. Our young students have practiced so much that they shoot first not only old rabbits but also very young ones just born." These are the words of Hans-Joachim Iwand, a leading German theologian in the fifties, spoken as part of some noteworthy peripheral remarks to his talk on "Responsibility and Tasks of Christians in the International Situation of Today."

Iwand presented his talk at the first Christian Peace

Conference in Prague, 1958. In it he captured a characteristic trait of the theological situation after World War II, above all, in Germany. Christian theology, both Catholic and Protestant, took a stand against ideology. Ideologies and their rule in society were seen as a serious threat to our concrete existence as human beings. Our fate was bemoaned, especially under the rule of so-called "totalitarian ideologies." Theologians and churchmen considered themselves challenged on this very point. Thus ideologies were theologically unmasked; the Word of God was understood as a "hammer against ideologies" and hurled down from many a pulpit.

The Christian contribution was seen in the reduction of ideologies in modern society.

IDEOLOGY AS TRANSFIGURATION OF REALITY   This negative attitude is not completely unfounded. Even more, it corresponds to a large part of the historical background of the concept of ideology itself, above all in German intellectual history. What is meant by ideology? In the third edition of *Religion in Geschichte und Gegenwart* (*Religion in History and the Present*) we read: "Ideology is a system of social thinking in which the trans-empirical categories and the choice of empirical material is influenced—if not totally determined—by the social interests and emotional attitudes of the observer. Hence the view of the observer regarding the world does not necessarily correspond to its structure, but rather it reflects his place in it." (N. Birnbaum). This is a descriptive and rather cautious definition. However, in it also is noticeable a certain distrust toward ideologies. The world of ideology is the world of emotions and interests, of conscious and unconscious tendencies, and therefore it is not objectively dependable.

This suspicion and this skepticism have often been expressed much more vigorously in the history of the concept. I do not think immediately of the Emperor Napoleon, one of the first and most radical opponents of ideology, who called ideologists simply "useless babblers," incapable of coping with reality. I think rather of the keen criticism that was brought out by the young Karl Marx with regard to this concept. Marx's view uses as a point of departure the unhappy situation of German philosophy after Hegel's death. He depicts the process of deterioration of the Hegelian system which, as he says, has developed into a world fermentation. "Powers of Chaos broke out; mighty empires were founded and toppled! Heroes without equals appeared—a revolution compared to which the French Revolution was child's play! Fights of the Diadochi about Hegel's large heritage. . . ." This ironic presentation is introduced with the words, "As German ideologists proclaim. . . ." It is found at the beginning of a work called *Deutsche Ideologie (German Ideology)*. In this manner a critique of ideology is inaugurated. It is utterly wrong to consider the Idea as something original and essential, as did those very post-Hegelian Diadochi. "Morality, religion, metaphysics, and other ideologies and their corresponding forms of consciousness herewith no longer retain their semblance of autonomy."

Hence, thinking is not sovereign; it depends on social reality. Therefore consciousness can in no way form the fulcrum of our life and thought. On the contrary, it is not only secondary but under given circumstances even unreliable. For the class society, as Marx formulated it later, ideology is an instrument of "false consciousness." It glosses over and transfigures reality in the interest of those in power. In this way ideology is tendentious. Ideological consciousness contradicts the spirit of objective cognition. Above all, it is a bulwark against the necessary change of society. It is an instrument of enslavement. And so ideology—under given circumstances—is principally unreliable.

Distrust toward ideology remained a part of German—and not only German—thinking. In fact it was generalized and absolutized, which was not the case with Marx, as we shall see. Nietzsche, for instance, understood ideology as a cloak of the true and only reality, namely the will to power. And for Freud the problem of our ideological consciousness was, in the final analysis, a problem of the strategy of the subconscious. Thus human ideology lay claim to no true authenticity. It is an instrument of deception.

If one then considers this critical tendency toward the concept of ideology which has been held among the leading thinkers of the European history of philosophy, it is no wonder that the word generally has a negative tone. We also have to take into consideration that this critical opinion—measured against the facts and experiences of social as well as personal life—has simply proved itself: How often have noble ideals and programs turned out, on closer inspection, to be a cover for much less noble interests (and Christians should not primarily think of others but of themselves in this area)! Thus that emphatic distrust of ideology among modern theologians is not entirely incomprehensible. It may make sense to discard in the social and private realm any naïveté regarding ideological constructs. It need not be viewed as a cynical attitude if one becomes distrustful toward the big pathos-laden words and ideals. It is a good thing to try to procure more space for concrete humanity to cross all ideologies. In this sense theological efforts on behalf of a deideologization of modern life are also to be regarded as a legitimate charge of the church—above all, when this happens not only with critical zeal but also with self-critical zeal. The reduction of ideologies within the church, both in message and in practice, is indeed our task.

If one were to try to summarize the reasons that might be adduced for the theological justification of this reticence regarding ideology, one could, in the light of what has already been said, mention three points:

1. Ideology is theologically dubious because it represents the temptation, cogently grasped by Marx, of transfiguring the reality of the world and man in an illusionary way. When it gives in to this temptation it tends to cover up, in an act of deception or self-deception, the real distress of society, and interferes with necessary remedial action. This way it can feed the spirit of self-justification. In the church, ideology endangers any act of *metanoia*, penitent rethinking, and hence endangers the renewal of the church. Christianity, wrapped in ideology, becomes the opiate of the people and for the people.

2. Ideology is theologically dubious in that it tends to stylize concrete man in the interest of a dogma, a doctrine, or a system, and sometimes even to sacrifice him. An *eidos,* image, is drawn and then often taken more seriously than man himself. Iwand grasped this trait of ideological thinking with great keenness by characterizing ideology as the "arrogation of the rule of the spirit over man, modeled after the rule man has achieved over nature or at least seems to have achieved over nature." In the church this mentality often is expressed in Pharisee-like legalism which regards a law as more important than man.

3. Ideology is theologically dubious also for a further special reason: it may attempt to generalize and to water

down the gospel—the message of God's concrete love for man in Christ—into a doctrine. The concrete acts of Jesus and the concrete testimony of the prophets and apostles are generalized ideologically, and an abstract *Weltanschauung,* embellished by Christian elements, is developed. In this way the word of the gospel loses its living edge and concrete moorings and is prepared, so to speak, for that exploitation mentioned in the first point, the exploitation of more or less nonevangelical interests.

A portion of the history of church dogma is, in this sense, really a history of ideology. The formation of dogma is not wrong in itself. In the earthly church, dogma is an unavoidable undertaking. However, in cases in which the dogma is severed from the living message (*kerygma*) and the living discipleship (*imitatio*), evangelical truth is transformed into an ideology. Examples: Romans 13 in the service of a conservative state ideology; the biblical-reformatory message of the grace of election ideologized into a component of capitalist mentality; the prolongation of the doctrine of two kingdoms into an evacuation of social life from the competence of the commandments of Jesus; the understanding of the Kingdom of Christ within the framework of a utopian enthusiasm. Thus "deideologizing" is a constant task of theology.

MEANS AGAINST HUMAN DISORDER AND AGAINST THE ORDER OF ANTS   And yet the cue word "reduction," as regards ideology, should not be our last word and, I should also say, not our first word. It would be a serious simplification of the problem of ideology if it were to be seen only in a negative light. From the point of view both of intellectual history and of theology this would not correspond to the facts. I should like to document this.

From the point of view of intellectual history. Up to now we have followed only one part of the background of the concept of "ideology," as far as intellectual history is concerned. Although it is the most exciting and, in some respects, the most interesting part, it is not the whole story. Hence it would be one-sided if, for instance, the conclusion were to be generalized that the content of the concept of ideology has altogether had a negative tone. This is refuted by the fact that the first coiners of this concept understood its content positively indeed. As is well known, it was a group of Frenchmen belonging to the later Enlightenment who designated themselves first as "ideologists," and their cause as "ideology." Above all, Destutt de Tracy, at the time of the French Revolution, in his *Science des Idées,* tried to find a scientific basis for social life by attempting to derive, by analogy to the natural sciences, a theory of society from an objectively dependable, scientifically satisfying source. This source was the perception of man's natural environment. Only ideas drawn from this source are able to scientifically shape society. Traditional concepts and prejudices, especially the metaphysical and religious ones, are to be put before the tribunal of genuine ideology and examined critically, if not ignored. In this way, ideology turns into an instrument of social reconstruction, into a positive phenomenon.

This positive view of ideology was, as we have seen, displaced by the negative one, but not replaced. This is particularly evident in the case of Karl Marx. Although in his critical analysis of German ideology there was a preponderance of sharp irony, even sarcasm, it was nevertheless clear to him that the positive potential of ideology is by no means eliminated. His pupils, especially V. I. Lenin, claimed this name for the ideology of the proletariat, that is to say for his philosophy. They were criticized for it from many quarters. Did not the keen critics recognize the "ideological" character (in the negative sense) of their own system?

Yet fundamentally, no objection is to be raised against an emphatic dialectic in the concept of ideology. In the realm of history there exist not only wrong ideologies but also right ones. This is understood by the Marxists in the following way: the moment when it corresponds to the interests of the future, a "false consciousness" is replaced by a positive ideology. Marx and his disciples were convinced that this is the case and that it happens in the ideology of socialist revolution at the end of the bourgeois epoch. Here is found the ideology of the future, and also the future of ideology. Ideology obtains decisive meaning in social reconstruction. It becomes the "light of social life." It leads men out of their blind tutelage; it integrates the forces of the new society. What a positive view of ideology! Thus, against the background of intellectual history alone an exclusively negative evaluation of the concept of ideology appears as one-sided and not justified.

This is also true with respect to theology. We have already pointed emphatically to the special dangers of ideological thinking from the theological standpoint; three points were made. These points retain their validity. Certainly, we will have to approach ideologies with soberness—not only according to Marx but also in the light of the gospel. Sobriety, however, does not mean diabolization; it also implies receptivity for possible positive elements. In one word, no "riflemen's festival," no "shooting parties." More reason for this needs to be given.

1. The "spirit of the riflemen's festival" concerning ideology is exactly what is theologically dubious. Almost

all shooting matches on this earth are suspicious, especially when, as Iwand said, "not only old rabbits," but rather "very young ones, just born," are hit. This, naturally, is the language of imagery. What is meant is the spirit of an undifferentiated antiattitude, of enmity from principle, and of pleasure in destruction.

It is exactly such an attitude as this that proves irresponsible. Like the mood of any crusade, any witch hunt, any cold war, the mentality of the riflemen's party does not correspond to the real essence of God's creation. It smells of Manichaeism, of a demonization of the world or part of the world. Such an attitude, to be sure, appears to correspond radically and profoundly to the biblical pronouncements regarding evil and to represent an uncompromising doctrine of sin. But it really does not. The deep seriousness of the Bible does not signify a diabolization of the world. To be sure, our world is a perverted creation. It is perverted by men. Hence let there be no illusions. However, our world is the perverted creation of God, of the faithful God who in his unconditional faithfulness does not give up his creation, not even in sin, not even when facing the devil. That is the reason why there is no reality on this earth that should be rejected without differentiation as the whole "species" (the "big and the very little rabbits").

2. This is generally true, and it is valid also in the particular case of human ideology. Theologically seen, what is an ideology? Certainly no angelic bridgehead in the world of creation. In the history of dogma such attempts at theological appreciation of the spirit and its manifestations are frequently undertaken; for instance, in conjunction with the *Imago Dei* doctrine. Is not at least a remnant of this image of God to be seen in human spirituality, materially or at least formally? I do not

agree to this. Barth's criticism of the traditional *Imago Dei* doctrine seems to be justified biblically. The idealistic interpretation of biblical anthropology misses the meaning of the decisive biblical statements. The spirit in itself is not the light (as the body per se is not darkness). The line of demarcation between good and evil does not simply run in favor of spirituality in the segregation of the anthropological components of a human being. We know that the human spirit, too, is deeply involved in the perversion. Therefore: no angelicizing of ideologies.

On the other hand, there also should be no demonization. Though the spirit is no angel, it is no devil, either. Though ideology is an enterprise full of risks, it is no enterprise that is condemned from the start. Ideology is a part of human reality, an element of human life. It is no more, but also no less. That sounds like a truism, but it is a statement of biblical-theological relevance. In that warning against riflemen's parties Iwand says simply, "I am of the opinion that man cannot live without ideology, and the reason for this is that we are not animals." This means that it is part of the structure of this creature called man that he is a thinking being and not an unthinking one. That is his potential. This is his risk. But at any rate, that is his way.

It is important to take this with sobriety. If one does not from the outset conceive of man "ideologically" in the negative sense, one cannot overlook the fact that man is an ideological being—a *homo ideologicus*. He lives thinking. He enters his world having thoughts about it; he tries to bring order into this world—his inner and his outer world—and to master it through thought. He lives in society by projecting his guiding images and following them more or less. Perhaps he deceives himself in this process; perhaps he is being deceived; perhaps he deceives others. But he thinks and seeks, and he probably finds. At any rate, he cannot help doing so. That is the condition of his life, especially of his social life. Human society is no anthill. Ideology is a means against human disorder and against the order of ants.

Here is the social locus of ideology. Man tries to integrate his communal existence. That is why ideology is to be taken seriously (like the state—*mutatis mutandis*). Certainly not with dead seriousness, not by absolutizing our ways, our thoughts, our ideologies, but critically; yet also frankly and without bias, like everything that is human. Theologically speaking, it is to be taken under the Judgment, but also under the Promise, in the christological perspective to which, for the sake of Christ, nothing human is alien. That is why those ideological riflemen are in error. It is true that with the ideology man is not hit at the same time. However, by showing hostility to ideology in principle, one shows hostility toward man. If ideology is not evaluated critically, with differentiation, but simply "slaughtered," then man, too, is endangered, and his world is disturbed. And that, from a christological perspective, is not justifiable.

3. A rejection in principle of ideology appears unjustified also for a third reason: it is borne, almost always, by the spirit of the law and not by that of the Good News. It is almost an irony that often an anti-ideological crusade is proclaimed in the name of the gospel. There is, however, the question whether this attitude does not endanger, or even surrender, the very cause it attempted to proclaim, namely the gospel itself.

What does it mean to launch an anti-ideological campaign? Does it not mean that one makes the Good News an anti-ideology, that one ideologizes it secretly and bends it into a law? Certainly, the gospel breaks any ideological spell. But this happens exactly in that it retains its "otherness" as the living voice of God (*viva vox Dei*). It is a word of salvation which includes all of man. It pertains also to the ideological sphere, but it does not simply coincide with it. Its kingdom is not the realm of ideologies. Therefore, neither can it be understood as an anti-ideology. Its encounter with ideology is of a different kind. In its light, ideology is recognized as ideology, as an image of the world and of society, and not as a word of salvation. However, the recognition of its relativity does not mean its abolition but its relative confirmation as a word of another, relative, worldly plane, legitimate in its secularity. In this way the gospel does not jealously erase ideology, but leaves faith free to integrate it—relatively—into the concrete context of the concrete reality of man. In this way, it remains Good News also with regard to ideologies and does not become law.

This differentiation of the gospel from ideological laws has still another side to it. It is meaningful not only in the interest of the gospel, but also in that of man. If one conducts an annihilation battle against ideologies, one does not help man exactly in the area in which one should like to protect him: against ideologization. For anti-ideology does not help against ideologization. Rather, ideologization is furthered by anti-ideology. Only man is a true limit to ideology: the fullness of man's existence in his history and his concrete expressions relativizes the "claim to totality" on the part of an ideology. Herein lies the tragedy of every idealism. The *eidos*, image, capsizes on reality. And herein is man's hope. He will never (in the sense of Iwand's words) be totally conquered by an ideology after the model of his own rule over nature.

This is also exactly the concern of the Good News of the way of God to man in Jesus of Nazareth. In its center does not stand an image of man, but man—Jesus, *Ecce homo*. Thus the act of witnessing to the gospel (and not anti-ideological resentment) is a bulwark against dangers of an ideological dogmatism (as was clearly proved by the concrete experiences of our churchly existence in the age of dogmatism). That is why it is important to stress that theologically, ideology must be approached from the basis of the Good News and not from law.

To summarize our trend of thought up to this point: Ideology is a function of being human. This is its justification. However, man is not a function of ideology. To overlook this is the temptation of ideology. In the preservation of this "dialectic," our theological service with regard to ideology occurs—or should occur. In other words, it is the witness of evangelical freedom which is to be expected from theology and the church with respect to ideology.

Therein is implied (to summarize our negative analyses): (1) freedom in the sense of a struggle for a genuine reduction of any false ideologization of modern life, freedom from "false consciousness," freedom from any dogmatically absolutized ideology, and above all, freedom to reduce ideology in the promulgation of the gospel. However, there is also implied (as the result of our positive considerations): (2) freedom in the sense of an evangelical, not legalistic openness to this legitimate part of human reality, to ideological life and striving.

Perhaps today this second aspect deserves special stress. If the saying by Iwand which was our point of departure is correct, our theology is threatened not so much by too great a sympathy for the ideologies of our world as rather inversely by a pronounced antipathy. This antipathy needs to be restrained. An anti-ideological complex, above all an acidulous distrust of any clearly pronounced ideology, constant attempts to unmask or refute it (I am thinking especially of the preponderantly prevalent attitude of theologians and also of parishioners toward Marxism), is no sign of theological integrity but is rather the opposite. The pioneering thoughts of Bonhoeffer with regard to the "world come of age" are also to be certified in the very difficult realm of ideological life. And that means free, critical, yet sympathetic solidarity, and positive dialogical participation in any serious, constructive, ideological work in our society.

TOLERANCE AND INDIFFERENCE   Here arises the question (and a skeptical question it is) which is to occupy us in conclusion, the question of ideology and tolerance. The question can be worded: Does one not deceive oneself in the theological effort of understanding ideology positively (especially when meaning a clearly formulated strong ideology)? Does not this effort endanger exactly that which we have formulated as the task of Christians in the field of ideology, namely, that dialogical participation in the thought and life of society? Any strong ideology tends toward exclusivity, claims a monopoly of rightness, and hence is militant. One may think especially of Marxist ideology. Does it not postulate, even when it proclaims the principle of peaceful coexistence on the international plane, that there cannot be any coexistence in the field of ideology? Does this not exclude tolerance and, since without a minimum of tolerance no genuine discussion can come about, likewise any possibility of that very "dialogical participation"? The problem of ideology and tolerance delineates itself in sharp contours. What is to be said of it?

If tolerance were a *laissez-faire* indifference, then, to be sure, any clear-cut ideology would be a threat—why, even the end of tolerance. For any real ideology stands there with its clear claim and thus is intolerant. However, does tolerance mean the same thing as indifference? At this point a reminder of the biblical background may be helpful.

In his St. John Commentary, Rudolf Bultmann, in conjunction with the explanation of the *"Ego Eimi"* (I am) of Jesus, formulates some significant thoughts pertaining to the question of tolerance. Among other things he writes, "The *Ego Eimi* of Jesus always means: there is only one leader to salvation, only one revealer. Regarding the question about salvation there are not different possibilities but only the one. A decision is requested. In that lies the intolerance of Revelation. To be sure, it is Revelation which is intolerant; human beings can only be tolerant with one another; and insofar as men have to champion the intolerant claim of Revelation, this claim is directed in the first place against themselves. The intolerance of the 'homo religiosus' and of the dogmatician is not the intolerance of Revelation."

This important distinction of Bultmann's shows that the Christian concept of tolerance is a truly dialectical one: tolerance toward men does not exclude intolerance in the question of truth, and vice versa. The two are to be distinguished. When no distinction is made, when tolerance toward man leads to a dilution of the question of truth, or when the intolerance of the claim to truth is extended into an intolerance toward one's neighbor, the biblical concept of tolerance is being distorted. Only in the tension of an absolute obligation to recognized and professed truth, and simultaneously an attitude of openness for those thinking differently, can biblical tolerance be understood.

It would, of course, be short-circuit reasoning to apply

this biblical view of the tolerance problem to the problem of ideology and tolerance directly. Bultmann stresses quite clearly that, in biblical intolerance, it is the intolerance of Revelation that is in question. Revelation is not ideology, and ideology is not Revelation. The claim to absoluteness of Revelation legitimizes no claim of absoluteness by ideology. And yet the biblical background, the structure of the biblical concept of Revelation, can help us gain a certain understanding of tolerance also in the field of ideology.

One thing is especially clear: tolerance is not *laissez-faire* toleration. It is not *indifferentia*—rather, it happens *in differentia,* in putting up with differences. "Tolerance in the broadest sense is to endure the other man in his otherness" (H. Gollwitzer). In a genuinely tolerant attitude, it is not a question of relativistically glossing over differences to weaken and minimize them. On the contrary, it is a question of facing them soberly and sharply. This is particularly true with regard to ideological otherness. Tolerance endures otherness, even challenges it for the sake of the truth, without which genuine tolerance does not exist. Even with his Quaker background, Richard Ullmann says rightly, "Tolerance is the real battle field on which the war for the truth must be ventured." And so, ideological struggling does not exclude real human tolerance, just as genuine tolerance does not exclude ideological battles.

The argument that a strong ideology endangers, and must endanger, human tolerance and genuine dialogue does not stand the test. We certainly do not need to conceal from ourselves the dangers of a strong, pronounced, and presumptuous ideology. Man will always be tempted to extend the intolerance of his zeal for truth, in a seemingly logical but essentially irresponsible manner, into a global intolerance; he will be tempted to suspect and to fight his ideological opponents as enemies per se and to carry on the ideological struggle with other means (in the extreme case to carry it to the point of physical liquidation). Exactly as Christians we do not underestimate the dangers of this odious logic of intolerance in any way. How often, in our own case, did a genuine intolerance of the faith in Revelation suddenly turn into the intolerance of an inquisition of one or another kind! And yet the claim to truth of Revelation was not refuted thereby. And so, *mutatis mutandis,* ideology itself is not discredited by the abuse of ideologists.

We may now come to the end and conclude: A church living in an ideologically exposed situation (as, for instance, the churches in the Marxist-socialist countries) will by no means have only to complain about the situation. Such a church will remain soberly aware of the special dangers of such a situation for itself and for society, and it will try to check them. However, it will also try to accept with an open mind the special opportunities, both for society and for itself. The truth of the gospel might be taken more seriously in such a situation than in other places where the church operates in a pluralistic-relativistic atmosphere. It can be taken more seriously, both by the opponents and by the confessors, with a greater sense of obligation against the "obligatory background" of an "obligatory ideology."

This theory is not one of consolation; it is a piece of our reality and of our experience as Christians in socialist society in the last decades. What an experience it can be in our situation to preach evangelically! In the final analysis this experience means the following: If theology and the church do not respond to a sharp ideological situation in their society with anti-ideological negatives, but prove their evangelical freedom by critically constructive participation in the questions arising from this situation; and if, in doing this, they commit themselves with concentration to the truth of the gospel, then the way opens, even in the face of a pronounced ideology, for a meaningful mission and service in the church and in society.

GOOD NEWS
FOR ATHEISTS

In 1958 Josef L. Hromádka published in Berlin a book called *Gospel for Atheists*. In it he attempted to develop one of the basic concerns and impulses of his theological work of the past decades: the task of a theologically legitimate encounter with the ideological and political representatives of his society—with the Marxists, the Communists, and thus the atheists. Hromádka's attempt was productive in many ways, and it broke open a new avenue of approach as he helped to inaugurate the "era of dialogue" between Marxists and Christians after years of mutual indifference. If I place my deliberations on the theme of "atheism" in line with the title of his book, I mean to indicate that I am here not presenting a general analysis of the phenomenon of atheism, but rather I approach the issue on the basis of practical and theoretical experiences of the past twenty years of our theological existence in a Marxist-socialist society. In this sense, I will try to sketch out some lines and perspectives as they have emerged from encounters with fellowmen in our radically secularized surroundings.

A DEMYTHOLOGIZING OF ATHEISM   The history of the encounters of the church with atheism is a history encrusted with prejudices and caricatures. It is replete with fixed battle lines and battle cries and marked by a mutual "demonizing" of the other side. That is true of both sides, also of the atheist side. How often European atheism dealt with the problem of religion more in the spirit of an embittered antagonism than in a soberly differentiating discussion!

Traces of such conduct existed even in ancient times— for example, in the pathos of Lucretius Carus, for whom the dissolution of religion and the arrival of Epicurean atheism almost signified a breakthrough on the way of liberation from basic human bondage and slavery. More traces of animosity are plainly evident in the various streams of militant "confessional" atheism in Europe of the last centuries. How frequent have been the charges by this atheism that religion is a "radical evil," that it is the root of all that is wrong! Such charges were launched by the freethinkers of the Enlightenment with their battle cry *"Ecrasez l'infâme!"* addressed against the institutionalized form of religion. In the nineteenth century, for Feuerbach the abolition of religion formed the fundamental presupposition of men's emancipation. Similarly Nietzsche considered his anti-Christian front as *the* way toward becoming the superman (*Übermensch*). Up until the present time many militant atheists have continued this tendency; even within the socialist society there were propagandists to whom the dissolution of religion became *the* task of the cultural revolution.

We Christians know very well this "catalog of sins" of atheists, and naturally we dismiss this uncritical, absolutized, oversimplified, even mythological way of thinking. But precisely in this connection it is necessary for us to understand and acknowledge that a similar way of thinking and dealing characterizes the church's encounter with atheists. With respect to the centuries-long power position of the church in the public life of the "Christian West" an antagonistic intolerance is even more conspicuous and disastrous. The history of the concept of atheism and the fate of atheists in European life and thought illustrates that at almost every step along the way.

From the church's point of view, obviously atheism is a negative phenomenon. It denies God and thereby very often as well threatens man. To recognize that fact in a sober and critical way and to discuss the matters at issue should also be a part of the church's encounter with atheists. But how rapidly has the appropriate critical relation toward atheism been uncritically expanded into a massive negativism! How quickly has European man within his Christian civilization resorted to summarizing atheism as something inhuman, absolutely perverted, yes, something almost demonic! So, for centuries the atheist has been regarded in public European (and American) opinion as someone basically irresponsible and, thus, untrustworthy and even immoral. Atheism itself has consequently been viewed in a juridical way as a sacrilege, a transgression, something which should be resisted with utmost retaliation, sometimes even to be atoned for with the death penalty. In this connection the argument might have emerged that it was better to destroy the body than to leave it unpunished, lest the soul become tainted and others contaminated.

The most crude forms of this mythologizing attitude toward atheists and atheism have vanished. The negative attitude nevertheless survived the Middle Ages. It can actually enjoy a certain renaissance in a new form, even evolving some politically organized forms. I am referring to the era of the Cold War. Didn't the problem of atheism play a considerable role in this unfortunate era? Didn't political contradictions become branded as religious, or better, as pseudo-religious? Didn't many speak too generally and too simply of the "Christian West" and the "atheistic East?" The political and social tension has been consequently radicalized to a final irreconcilable breach. It has taken on the character of an eschatological struggle of the children of light against the children of darkness. The most dangerous means of mass destruction which politicians had at their disposal were justified on the basis of these mythological categories. For example, churchmen could defend the pseudo-theological argument that "death of the soul" (meaning atheistic ideology) is more serious than physical death (even when inflicted by the atom bomb). This mythology of the Cold War has become to some degree discredited and destroyed today. But *vestigia terrent*. Therefore it seems advisable also on this very practical ground to try to demythologize the categories we employ in our confrontation with atheism.

What does that really mean? I would say first it means

simply to recognize and acknowledge the relativity of atheism. I want to explain this idea in its historical, psychological, and theological aspects.

1. *The historical relativity of atheism.* We should not overlook the fact that the concept has been expressed and applied in many different ways. The concept in itself is naturally Greek, and its various meanings are evident already in antiquity. The Greeks designated as atheist not only those declared deniers of God and the materialists but also those who in the name of another faith (and that can mean a belief in another god) separated themselves from the established religion. Most of the struggles with atheists were of this type. Just think of Socrates!

Such a procedure was then applied to the Christians, because in the Hellenistic world they were *atheoi,* atheists. "Down with the atheists!" was subsequently the battle cry which many a Christian martyr encountered! But the sword point was quickly reversed, Christians held the handle as they charged the heathen. One need only read the story of Polycarp's martyrdom. This martyr was pressed to deny his Christian faith with the cry "Down with the atheists." He spoke these words indeed—but in a clear reference to his own heathen opponents.

And not only against the heathen was this idea pressed into service in the course of the church's history. Even professing Christians were condemned as "atheists" by the then reigning orthodox party. We need only recall the Inquisition and the Crusades and the confessional battles of different types. Whoever reflects on all that, and more precisely, whoever remembers the simple fact that even his forefathers in the faith were designated by the term "atheist" and persecuted by it, should be quickly stopped in using the notion of atheist in an all-too-hasty and inconsiderate way. He should hesitate to use it as a denouncing shibboleth in an absolutizing and mythological manner. It is worthwhile to remember this lesson of our historical orientation and resist that inquisition and crusade spirit precisely when we meet those who think differently from us, especially in our encounters with atheists.

2. *The psychological relativity of atheism.* What I want to refer to with this concept is, to start with, the fact that atheism as unbelief does not generally represent a metaphysically petrified stage in the history and historicity of human life, but rather a dialectical phase of life. It often emerges in the course of the life of faith as a "not yet" or a "no more" of believing. "I believe, help my unbelief" (Mark 9:24). Now this situation is significant. Whoever understands such relativity will not be so easily tempted to consider the atheistic possibility as something totally alien to him, as a curse which only drives and threatens other men. He will not be able to dissociate himself from this possibility in a self-confident and self-secure way. He will not forget that all men, the pious and the worldly, here find themselves together in the same situation. In the past centuries of an almost natural and normative presupposed religiosity it might have been possible to disregard or to conceal this fact. It has become much clearer today for a thinking contemporary with regard to the process of secularization concerning all of us—the religious men and the secular men.

3. The acknowledgment of the *theological relativity of atheism* directs us even further, to the foundations of the life of faith as understood by the Bible. In this view atheism is no absolute position, no beginning or new beginning, no real creative act; rather, it is something secondary, a reply, a reaction. This is, of course, no historical, phenomenological, or general philosophical assertion. It is an expression of faith which testifies that the beginning

and ground of human existence does not lie within us (not even in our faith!) but lies instead in the reality which is the basis for faith—in the reality, action, and history of God. The "essence of Christianity" is founded not by faith but by the work of God—more exactly, in the life, death, and resurrection of Jesus Christ. Thus this "essence" of faith cannot in any way be destroyed by unfaith. Both faith and unfaith are not the "matter itself" (although they are never to be separated from this "matter"), but instead they are a response to it. As such they are to be taken seriously, for this "matter" presses for a corresponding response, it calls for faith, and it repudiates unfaith. It is not a matter of indifference if we give one reply instead of another. In this respect there can be no relativism. And yet the gospel is not simply contained within these replies. It is not dependent on them. The gospel remains sovereign over faith and unfaith.

The structure and movement of biblical history points in this direction. We consider the covenant Jahweh made with Israel already in the Old Testament. Of course, this covenant appeals to the faithfulness of the covenant community. The people's unfaithfulness toward the covenant is never calmly accepted. Instead, it is again and again uncovered, accused, and rejected. But the glory of God is never frustrated, even when God gets no appropriate answer. The glory of God manifests itself exactly in the fact that he himself stands by the covenant even when that covenant is broken by his people.

This basic emphasis of the biblical witness achieves final and overpowering clarity in the New Testament. In facing the cross of Jesus Christ, unfaith is revealed in its total failure; its harmfulness is unmasked and condemned. But beneath the cross of Jesus Christ the unbeliever is received into the unconditional solidarity of God with estranged man. The real situation of mankind is brought to light: every one of us lives (whether we know it or not, whether we admit it or deny it) beneath the sign of the cross and the resurrection. We live on the supporting ground of the saving solidarity of God. That is the decisive, truly constitutive fact of human existence according to the Bible. That is the Good News. Man is to be regarded in the light of this Good News. With his answer—and also with his atheism. His denial appears in the Bible only against this background, as something secondary, perverted, but also as something already overcome by God's faithfulness. So atheism is not a hopeless ultimate step but is something penultimate, and in that sense, relative.

What I mean by the theological relativity of atheism is that the sovereignty of the Good News of Jesus Christ is above all human action and omission, even above man's faith and unfaith. "At the right time, while we were still helpless, Christ died for the *ungodly*[!]" (Romans 5 :6). In this view atheism is not simply disregarded; it is demythologized.

ENCOUNTER IN THE LIGHT OF THE GOOD NEWS   The task of the church is to declare the Good News. That is its proper obligation, what it owes the men of its world. As the apostle Paul said about his work (almost previewing his mission), "I am under obligation both to Greeks and to barbarians, both to the wise and to the foolish. So I am eager to preach the gospel to you also who are in Rome" (Romans 1 :14–15). On other similar occasions Paul affirmed that the witness of the gospel was the one ground and goal of his labors. In naming the recipients of his testimony, he mentioned the Greeks *and* barbarians, the wise *and* the foolish, and of course the Jews *and* the heathen. These were the most evident dividing lines in the society of his time. Nevertheless, he asserted that the one thing that was necessary, and necessary for all, was to preach the Good News to *everyone*. The exclusive theme, the gospel, is unexpectedly inclusive. It spans every chasm and separation. It concerns everyone: the pious Jew and the impious (or pseudo-religious) heathen; the true theist and those who from the point of view of the pious necessarily appear to be atheists. The apostle is obligated also to these persons. In our apostolic discipleship that is, therefore, our task and our responsibility: to preach the *Good News even to atheists*.

It is surprising that Christians and their organized churches have so frequently forgotten these apostolic footsteps in their relations with atheists; instead of preaching an "inclusive" gospel, they have many times preached and preached an "exclusive" excommunicative law. Thus it frequently happens that atheists themselves understand better than Christians something of the spirit of the *Good News*. For example, the Czech Marxist philosopher Milan Machovec interpreted the message of the gospel (incidentally, a message which, as he often said, inspired him throughout his life) as being concerned for people in the following way: "I could swear that millions of modern men, who are deeply aware of something like an anti-religious *a priori*, are still my brethren, who are not excluded from the message of Christ, that he is merciful to people." Here a Marxist thinker understands that the solidarity of Jesus is inclusive, that it includes even those who are severely estranged from him. How often has this central confession been lacking among Christians! So it could possibly be (and it would not be strange within the context of the story of Jesus of Nazareth) that the heathen and the estranged might be nearer the Kingdom than many of the righteous!

But what does this "Good News for atheists" really mean in our encounter with our atheistic fellowmen? Which perspectives can be thereby opened up? What proceedings are thus indicated for us to initiate an authentic encounter? In a preliminary way I want to answer these questions with the following proposition: The encounter of Christians with atheists will proceed correctly on the part of the church only when it is done in the spirit of the Good News and not in the spirit of the law. On the basis of what I have said thus far, I want to develop briefly in three comments what this proposition means.

1. To proceed in the spirit of the Good News means first to proceed in the *spirit of freedom.* The gospel is the message of the sovereign freedom of God, and included in that is the freedom of the Christian man. On that basis the element of freedom should be preserved in our encounter with atheists. I have already indicated how the conduct of Christians throughout the past and in these present times leaves much to be desired in this respect. Recall the first part of these deliberations, when I showed how often Christians negotiated with the "ideological adversary" much more on the basis of law than on the basis of the Good News! The adversary became "mythologized." But that procedure will take its toll. Freedom is lost in the process, for whenever I mythologize the other person I give up my freedom with reference to him. Over against a demon a man is not free. Demons are fate-laden principalities and powers and are unfathomable. There is no encounter with them. Conversation is no longer possible. Facing what is demonized places one in a position of enforced choice. There are only two possibilities: retreat into a closed-off cell or exorcize the demon!

These two alternatives were often practiced during the church's history. The possibility of pulling back into a closed-off sector is seen in the withdrawing of a sacred precinct, the tearing down of the bridges to the world, and the establishing of prickly defenses by the ghetto church. The strategy of exorcism is developed in demonizing atheism, in launching crusades against it. Both ways are mistaken. What we allegedly want to save, evangelical freedom (the freedom of the gospel), is threatened by both sides. For freedom exists only when, believing in the sovereignty of the Good News, we seek and reach the other person, proceeding soberly, circumspectly, critically, but with openness toward him. The element of such a kind of freedom is the first condition and the primary sign of a confrontation with atheists in conformity to the gospel.

2. To proceed in the light of the Good News and not on the basis of law means *not to begin first at the level of ideology*. It is important to guard against an ideologization of the encounter, which corresponds to the spirit of law. The spirit of the gospel completely breaks through all ideological barriers. It leads from ideology to the man.

That does not necessarily mean a devaluation of ideology, neither underestimating nor demonizing it. As pointed out in the preceding chapter, ideology is a part of human existence. It is a significant part. It is a phenomenon which among other things raises man above the animals. It is a guiding star or a guideline for human life and actions. Yet it is not the whole of human existence; it is not a sum total of that which is human, and it is not, without qualification, man's very essence. In any case, a man is not exhaustively contained in his ideology. He is more than what he thinks. He is more than an "-ist," a the-ist, athe-ist, or any other kind of -ist. He transcends all his "-isms."

With reference to our meeting atheists this assertion means that assuredly such an encounter has an ideological aspect. It would be dishonest and unhuman to forget that.

We *are* obligated to atheists to carry on an ideological discussion. We also have to orient members of our congregations and our Christian young people in the beliefs of atheistic ideology. *But* we must not consider this mandatory task as the "first and the last." It is something second or penultimate. It is *not* the Alpha and the Omega. In the light of the Good News about the incarnation of the Son of God, *man* is important, not his ideology. We do not mean that we have fulfilled our obligation to atheists when we have only ideologically questioned and denied their atheism.

If we deceive ourselves at this point, we may barely miss having an authentic encounter. Ideology becomes more important than the man. And what is more disastrous is that the Good News becomes obscure to the atheist. The gospel's divine and human sovereignty is diminished if it is confined (perhaps in our apologetic zeal) to the ideological level of approach. The Good News becomes ideologized, turned into an ideology or counterideology. Under certain circumstances that may appear to be tempting—when, for example, the gospel becomes a tool ready to do battle against vulgar antireligious propaganda. We might even achieve some "victories" in the ideological conflict. *But* such a success is even in the best circumstances something like a sham victory and ultimately a definitely ambiguous "success." For in these ways, the Good News is eclipsed—also for atheists. The one thing we really owe to the atheist is the message about the sovereign love of Christ. That love shatters every ideological barrier in order to seek and find man. To seek and find the Christian and the heathen, the pious and the worldly, the theist and the atheist. And that is why we say the way leads from ideology to the man himself.

3. To encounter another person in the light of the

Good News and not on the basis of law means that we are to meet him in the *spirit of solidarity* and not in an attitude of self-righteousness. The legalistic attitude implies self-assertion and self-righteousness, and because of that it is basically an antagonistic conduct. The "righteous ones" stand up *against* the others. Yet the way of the gospel is being for others, the way of proexistence. We can put it this way: Proexistence is the basic form of an evangelical existence whenever it meets a fellowman, and that includes the atheist. Proexistence learns to give up every self-justification and to understand the other man in his need and in his concern. There is also an intellectual aspect to this—a careful differentiating attempt to understand another's proper aims and intentions. As I tried to show earlier when I spoke of a demythologization of atheism, atheism is not something utterly foolish, nor is it an offspring of hell. Of course, atheism also *is* something foolish, and I mean that in the profoundly biblical (nonmoralizing) sense (see Psalm 14:1). A history of atheism could be written on that basis. But it could be discussed in an entirely different way, and that way is more useful and interesting for the Christian! Atheism can be understood as a reply to the historical unfaithfulness and guilt of the established church.

This is very evident when we think of the major atheists in the history of the Christian church. They have been largely the voices of protest against abuses which should have been attacked and abolished in the light of the gospel. For example, consider Marx's atheism. It was a passionate protest against a religion and a church which had placed under a bushel the prophetic and apostolic light and example, neglecting especially man's social life. Religion and the church supported oppressive rulers and deceptively comforted the oppressed. In this connection the early Karl Marx should be read carefully. His was an atheistic protest, but one which bore in its atheism elements which have to be emphatically championed from the point of view of prophetic faith. How could we self-righteously and confidently face this kind of atheism—as well as the criticism of religion expressed by so many thinkers of European history, including countless fellow-men of our present era? How could we see in such atheism only darkness and the lack of human possibility? How could we dare to present our own tradition and achievements as utterly superior? Isn't atheism also a thorn in the flesh of a sleeping Christendom, a question to the church, a questioning of us, an inquiry into how we are Christians, an inquiry into just what we have done with the Good News?

Of course, we also have to put some questions to atheistic humanism from the side of the gospel, to ask especially whether the way of atheism does not threaten the very thing it seeks to preserve, that complete undiminished humanity of man. We have to ask whether precisely in its atheism it has not cut short the horizon of human hope. But such questions cannot be posed by "self-righteous possessors" (*beati possidentes*); they must be asked by those who sit "on the same bank" with all other men, together with them in their need and joined with them, too, in the hope given by the gospel—the Good News even for the atheists.

SOCRATIC WITNESS   We come finally to this question: Practically speaking, how does such a perspective worked out here relate itself to the encounter with atheists? Does "Good News for atheists" really work? Or is this purely a theological concept? Perhaps it is just a virtue from necessity; we in the church are driven up against the wall by modern atheism. We are in no position of strength to start retaliation. So we attempt a flight forward and call out that there is "Good News for atheists."

Admittedly we cannot simply dismiss these questions, especially when we look back carefully on the last twenty years' experiences. Certainly it is not easy to enumerate statistically the positive results. Attempts to adopt a new church orientation toward atheism have not led to any mass conversions. Surely we can cite some real conversions, yet they are almost always an exception. They are "miracles," signs, but no conclusive proof.

Nevertheless, one can point to one phenomenon to show that the perspective of "Good News for atheists" is not merely a motto. I refer to the phenomenon of dialogue between Christians and atheists as it has begun and developed in the last years. With this concept of dialogue I come now to a significant point. So far in this chapter I have not explicitly touched on it, but it is the point which has been intended from the beginning: the intention of or effort to demythologize atheism, to dissolve fixed positions, to cast off the historical ballast—to do all this precisely for the sake of making possible a dialogical encounter. With the same intention I emphasized Good News and not law in our conversations with atheists; it is a matter of making room for an authentic encounter, one in line with the gospel, making way for a credible witness. Our theological work of the past decades has been developed into this aim—to open the possibilities of dialogue.

The following section will concentrate on this issue. It will show that indeed a new realm opened for a Christian witness in the atheistic environment. It is still narrow, but its perspective looks promising to us.

I have titled these concluding remarks with the phrase "Socratic witness." This motto, used by Dr. Willem Visser't Hooft at the Fourth Conference of European Churches held in Nyborg, describes the narrow but still hopeful way of Christian witness in the radically secularized world of the European West and East. He defined the way as an evangelism in which the evangelist does his service "more as a midwife" than as a distributor of authoritative solutions.

In this sense of the word we as Christians try to serve in our society. Not as those who possess all the truth, not as ideological masters who teach and know everything better, but as those who share the concerns and expectations of their fellowmen and endeavor to help with the one thing which is necessary for us all, the Good News for atheists.

CHRISTIAN-MARXIST DIALOGUE

A NEW FASHION ?　　Christian-Marxist dialogue seems to have become a fashionable theme in contemporary European thought. As with all fashions, a critical question has to be faced: Is this really a meaningful, relevant, seriously worthwhile enterprise? The question may be asked from the *intellectual* point of view: Christianity and Marxism are two important overall thought systems. They are fixed and sufficiently developed; they cover practically all fields of human thought and life. Can these two intellectual networks meet at all? Are they not, in their evident (or pretended) self-sufficiency, basicly disinterested in other possibilities and therefore mutually exclusive? Especially when their basic philosophical starting points seem to be diametrically opposed—and therefore incompatible.

This hesitation may become more pronounced when one considers the peculiar and paradoxical *social* situation in the background of a Christian-Marxist dialogue. In the East, Marxists are the ruling group—with all the privileges and institutional (and sometimes administrative) power of official ideology, whereas Christians seem to be the underdogs. In the West, Christianity, though today with a less exclusive claim, has similar advantages, while Marxists seem to be the underprivileged. Can there be a real encounter under such circumstances? Isn't it bound to be always a hobbling—and that means a rather equivocal —eventually even dishonest dialogue? Possibly a slightly refreshing intellectual game, yet not quite a serious, relevant matter. Therefore, is it, strictly speaking, a really meaningful idea?

Let me say quite clearly: It is indeed a very real and relevant theme and a meaningful endeavor. I state this with deep personal conviction. For many of us, both Marxists and Christians, the intensity and depth of our mutual encounter has become one of the most encouraging experiences of the last years. Intellectually, the discovery that we have a great deal to say and contribute to each other—in spite of all our radical ideological differences. And socially, a new level of mutual understanding and even solidarity between many Christians and Marxists as it has emerged with unique intensity in Czechoslovakia in recent years in our common effort for humanization of our socialist society. From the perspective of this experience there is no doubt that encounter is a very real and relevant theme.

The warmth of this statement (or rather confession) is colored by the realization that this dialogue is by no means a matter of course. The skeptical questions we started with are not artificial—on both levels. In certain periods there was virtually no chance of a genuine and meaningful encounter. Certainly, the very genius of Christianity and Marxism moves toward, and inspires, dialogue. Both are basically "dialectical" and "eccentric." They know that the very structure of the world of man is a dynamic one and, consequently, that the way of human understanding and truth is always the way of encounter. And they also know that their own intellectual networks, the systems of their findings and beliefs, cannot remain in an ivory tower of a proclaimed self-sufficiency, that they have again and again to transcend themselves. Thus the spirit of authentic Christianity and of authentic Marxism *is* the spirit of dialogue.

Yet as we all know, both these spiritual movements have had their periods of rigidity and dogmatic integralism. Both built their systems of ivory towers (and sometimes iron towers), and both were tempted—especially by the paradoxical power situation in which they were caught up in our divided world—either to silence or to disregard each other. If they met, they did so in a spirit of ideological militancy. So they preferred to launch the crusade against each other rather than to open a dialogue.

The traces of that rigidity and that crusade mentality are still on our faces and our ideas as we have gradually emerged out of the deep trenches of cold war periods in the last decades. Occasionally even some new such traces appear. Thus the Christian-Marxist dialogue is thus far not an "establishment," a firmly established institution. Its way is still a towaway zone—not quite safe for parking. It is a way of pilgrims and pioneers or of frontiersmen—not of functionaries and hierarchs (even when occasionally a Cardinal or a Politburo man may participate in the dialogue). In a word, it is still in process and progress.

PRESUPPOSITION OF A DIALOGUE: CONVERGENCE AND DIVERGENCE   A significant *convergence* between Marxism and the Christian message first became clear for some Christians and Marxists in practical matters. I am referring to the practical experience such as we have gathered in our society in the past decades. Christians and Marxists have been brought closer together in the decisive moments of our recent history in spite of the ideological tension and distance separating one from the other.

It was no accident that the intensive contacts of some theologians (J. L. Hromádka was foremost among them) had begun with Marxist leaders during the 1930's in a cooperative action to strengthen Spanish democracy. Christians and Marxists stood in common resistance to Fascism. They also participated in the common task of social reconstruction and the democratization of the socialist society.

This advance was intentionally impelled by practical and political motives. Both sides understood that there was no ideological identity. On the contrary, the ideological front remained unmoved. Yet practical cooperation precipitated a look into a certain convergence between the Christian message and Marxism. It was evidently not an accident that Christians and Marxists found themselves aligned in many practical decisions. They did not reach their analogous decisions haphazardly but on the basis of their faith and thought. This implied that they, at least, were deployed and motivated in a similar direction.

Thus it seemed very natural that they should clarify in a kind of mutual dialogue what this convergence (and what the persistent divergence) was all about.

In recent times from both sides has emerged the concept of *humanization* to characterize this shared concern of Christians and Marxists. This is certainly justified; humanizing social conditions is clearly our common concern. Still this concept is very general. If we are not able to fill this general idea with a more concrete content, the concept of convergence will be too narrow. Indeed, when we consider the exact meaning of humanization, especially when dealing with the question of what belongs to the "dimensions of the humane," the consensus between Marxism and the Christian message is much broader.

If I were to express this convergence in a very fragmentary and abbreviated way, using three major topics, I would select the concepts of society, history, and the future. The Marxist and Christian view of man emphatically states, to start with, that *man is a social creature*. Man is not an abstract, isolated creature content in himself. He lives in association with others. He is a social being. That is the fundamental qualification of his existence, and that is the delimitation of his being as a man. He has to be in an actual solidarity with other men, not bound up in concern for his own individuality only. That is the way of human fulfillment in a personal and social sense. Above all, that solidarity means fellowship with the poor and oppressed, the weary and heavy-laden— including the concern for a more just society. This stance of solidarity, this "socialistic impulse," distinguishes Christianity and Marxism from other orientations that place more emphasis on individual possibilities.

There is another shared attitude: *We both take history seriously* as a significant dimension of human existence.

Man is not an abstract, general, metaphysically prefabricated substance. He is a historical creature. By that I do not mean that he is an abstract individual, possessing "historicity," but rather that he exists and participates within the concretely given historical conditions and relations. Living in this historical context, he is no mere object in history; he is also history's subject and agent. History is his sphere of responsibility. History is the forum in which his business is transacted.

In this connection we come to the third shared concept: Christian and Marxist thought is *thinking directed to the future.* Man is *homo viator,* man on the way. He is on his way to a future destination. He is not tied down to a once-for-all-time given status quo. On the contrary, his heart belongs to that which will come. What is at hand is not enough for him. He must think about the promises of a greater justice. And in the light of that greater justice, he must not only interpret but change his world.

None of these converging motifs shared by Christians and Marxists can be simply stated without some qualification. None of these motifs excludes rather divergent aspects of these conceptions. What Marxism and the Christian message have in common under the topics of society, history, and the future is not identical. Therefore, when we think of the dialogue between the two, we must always consider the serious tensions between them.

Nevertheless, what I have indicated about the convergence between them is not an illusion. Their concentration upon these dimensions of man's existence clearly differentiates them from many other possible philosophical, religious, and political analyses of man, for example, the existentialist and the positivistic perspectives. Such a concentration makes them closely related partners of an authentic dialogue and social cooperation.

There is, as already indicated, a serious *difference* between Marxism and the Christian message. If I were to define more closely the decisive difference, I would cite the *question of God*. I recognize that precisely this difference can be viewed as an outmoded and consequently superseded recognition. Does the question of God really draw a genuine boundary line between Marxism and the Christian message? Hasn't theology today become quite cautious and hesitant exactly in this respect? Does the concept of God really belong to the "essence of Christian faith"? Many theologians today ask these questions.

From the other side, paradoxically, this question seems to be less fixed than ever. The saying that "God is not entirely dead" is heard from Marxist quarters, and from conversations with them we learn that the concern for transcendence is taken quite seriously by many present-day Marxists. Does the fundamental difference really rest on this point?

If I answer this question affirmatively, then I must hasten to add that in the "question of God" I do not refer to a metaphysical concept of God that we must establish as an absolute boundary over against the historical, dynamic, and social orientation of Marxist thought. Such a metaphysical concept would be a completely false boundary. The God of whom I am speaking is not the God of the philosophers, but the God of Abraham, Isaac, and Jacob.

Consequently, God is not the God of a metaphysical scheme but the God of history, of society, of the future— all in the concrete sense of the gospel of God's way for mankind in Jesus Christ. That is a transcendence that does not alienate man, one that does not divest man of his historical and social dimension, one that *does* free him for history, for social life, for the future. Furthermore, this transcendence is what sets the situation of man in a new light—the light of grace.

That is what I mean by the question of God: *the transcendence of grace.* Marxism disavows the question of God, seeing in it an improper turning away from man's concrete and worldly obligations. In view of the misuse of religion in the course of history, Marxism has solid grounds for its atheism. Dedication to the great task of the revolutionary refashioning of this world must not be watered down with "pious reasons." Christians should fully understand that, too. The gospel treats the world in utter seriousness. At the center of the gospel stands the proclamation of the *incarnation* of God. But exactly and specifically, it is the incarnation of *God.* If God is ideologically denied, man is threatened to become dissolved in his history, his society, and his future, and he becomes imprisoned in his immanence and his worldly projects. The penultimate becomes the ultimate for him. His total destiny then depends on his accomplishments. He lives with the possibilities of happiness and euphoria as they emerge in moments of his successes. But he also lives in frustration and despair as they are given in the situation of defeat and guilt.

Over against all of this the Christian message speaks of the transcendence of grace as the ultimate dimension of human existence. The *transcendence*: man is never used up completely in his social and historical conditions. His future is greater than the future of his accomplishments. He is more than he is. And the Christian message speaks of *grace*: our salvation is not related to our efficiency or the failure of our attempts. Our accomplishment is not what is ultimate. The ultimate is not our sin—so, too, it is not death for us. The ultimate, the proper future of man, is grace.

The real task of Christians in their encounter with Marxists appears to me to be to testify to this condition of being human. The church's mission lies exactly in this witness—in all societies, especially in a Marxist society. This is her authentic difference from the society; it is a difference that does not set her at a distance from others but one that unites her with them in Christian solidarity, a practical proof of the transcendence of grace. If the church fashions and promulgates laws instead of this message, she understands herself as an ideological anti-power set against Marxism (and how often she has done so!). If she does that, she misses her unique and most distinctive contribution and witness for society; she becomes worthless salt.

THE PROCESS AND PROGRESS OF THE DIALOGUE   Despite the potentialities of theoretical convergence and practical cooperation, the first years of Christian-Marxist coexistence in a socialist society (in a sense, the first century of their cohabitation in the broader context of European history) were characterized by a rather cool atmosphere of mutual segregation. Both camps were in their trenches and behind their fences, and their occasional communication was laden with mistrust and enmity. Both had their "good reason" for this attitude—that is, their own ideological stereotypes and fixed images. For many Christians, Marxists were basically atheists and materialists—the declared enemies of all Christian religion and order. And nearly all Marxists envisaged Christian churches as sheer obstacles to all progress and enlightenment.

The way from an anathema to dialogue had been long and difficult under these circumstances. One of its presuppositions was some success in *deideologizing the situa-*

tion; that is, in questioning the ideological stereotypes and shibboleths.

For us Christians this had two different aspects. One was a careful attempt to study what Marxism really was in its deepest possibilities and inspirations. This was not always easy—under the rule of a rather dogmatic and sterile form of orthodox Marxism with which we were confronted. But precisely in this respect it became our obligation not to identify the given ideological image with all possibilities of Marxism. In other words, we had to "deideologize" the Stalinist version and to seek for Marxism's human, original, and authentic face. In this effort, we developed a concentrated study of the young Karl Marx. It is interesting to note that the theologians started this study considerably earlier than the Marxists themselves. In the early fifties our Comenius Faculty in Prague was probably the only place in Eastern Europe where this deep humanistic philosophy was dealt with—as a challenge to the church first but also as a challenge to that Stalinist form of Marxism which was then the only form officially recognized. We did it not against the Marxists —as an act of ideological battle; on the contrary, we did it for them—or better, in our common interest of humanization of our society and as a presupposition for future dialogue.

A still more important aspect of the deideologizing was a concentrated effort to build up a "new reality" of Christian life and thought—in other words, to remove some obstacles for the Marxists in helping them to deideologize their own images of Christianity. What do I mean by this? According to the traditional Marxist conception, religion is either a superstition or a justification of class interests. If we look back into the situation in the nineteenth century (which Marx as a historically thinking political philosopher had primarily in mind), we have to acknowledge that this vision was very much justified. Christian thought and life were to a high degree hit by this criticism. Consequently, as long as the church embodies the spirit of superstition or of social reaction she has no chance of a real response to this criticism. She may launch many ideological crusades, and she may in many respects be right, yet she will hardly be credible. There will always remain a credibility gap.

Our basic task was precisely to overcome positively that credibility gap—in our context, to build up our church life in such a way that it would positively meet both levels of Marxian criticism. That implied two major concerns:

1. To elaborate a critical theology to meet the danger of superstition. Not to give in to the temptation of a fundamentalist ghetto mentality—to check the defensive, self-centered attitude which tries simply to keep what it has. We had to face and ask the questions of our secularized environment, to acknowledge the problems of demythologization, and to interpret the gospel to modern man. An intensive theological effort developed on these lines in our theological schools and even in our parishes. We might speak of a certain boom of Czech Protestant theology in this respect.

2. In meeting the question of a reactionary illusionism we had to face the reality of a new socialist society. We had to overcome a bias against this society. Such bias was strong among the Christians, because of the society's proclaimed atheism and because of its absolutizing claims. We had to be open for its experiments and ready to support it whenever it was acceptable from the Christian point of view. This especially meant not to "look back in anger" and not to bind our case with the ancient order

but, on the contrary, to welcome the basic structure change of socialist society and try to develop its human possibilities. The church had to be shaped not as a potential fifth column but as a new church in a new society.

It is easy to formulate such tasks in general terms. It is more difficult to translate this program into concrete steps of everyday Christian existence. In this we certainly did not always succeed. Yet something of that new reality emerged. We have become basically the church of our society. We were evidently something other than a dying-out handful of obsolete and superstitious people. And we were certainly not a fifth column of reactionaries trying to preserve social, economic, or cultural privileges. As a matter of fact we have lost nearly all of these historical privileges. This was bitter. But exactly in this area a new chance arose, the chance of a possible challenge to the traditional Marxist stereotypes of the church and of religion. A new church functioned as a question mark, inciting an endeavor toward a more differentiating attitude. In all this there was a clear invitation to dialogue.

We hoped that this invitation would not be totally overlooked or rejected. We had no guarantees for this hope. The possibility that Marxists would misunderstand our effort was not excluded. Was the Christian stand more than a new tactic, an attempt at desperate accommodation? Indeed it was a long time before the Marxists responded. Even some of the committed pioneers of dialogue among the Marxists hesitated for some time. They respected the social stance of some progressive Christians, but they suspected a certain inconsistency in their progressive attitude. They recognized them *in spite* of their Christianity and not *because* of that Christianity. This was clear, for instance, in the first judgments of Milan Machovec (who later became a passionate protagonist of the dialogue) about J. L. Hromádka. Machovec certainly recognized Hromádka as a progressive Christian citizen, but he was critical of him as a Christian. Nevertheless, the process of reevaluation started.

In this situation we were encouraged by a fundamental creative *process* of *reorientation* which was developing within the "other camp." In the later fifties new problems arose for sensitive and searching young Marxists. Such queries were evoked by a deep change in the overall cultural and social situation. The basic structural changes in our socialist society had been radically performed. The socialist basis was firmly established. The house of a new society was built. But what about the new man in that new house? The question of man emerged with a new and radical urgency.

This question had been rather neglected in the past. For the mainstream of Stalinist orthodoxy, it had a flavor of a typical bourgeois mentality. So it was left far behind the problems of structural social change. One of the official slogans of that era kept claiming: "The final aim of all our endeavor is man." But this "final" was somehow ambiguous. For many it was understood as a possibility to "bracket out" the question of man, to leave it really—for the end.

A typical axiom of dogmatic thinking strengthened this tendency of postponing the anthropological problem. The change within the economic basis, so it was claimed, would basically solve all the problems of superstructure, including the problem of ethics and of personal destiny. Is it, however, possible simply to postpone the question of man—especially if the basic structural change has already occurred? Is it not time to open the problem of man with a new urgency? What is the meaning of life? What is the goal of history—also of my own personal history? And what about the problem of evil—is the mystery of evil solved altogether by changing the structure of society and by establishing the new social order?

The old dogmatic system did not provide a convincing context for these questions. In its rigid and objectivistic framework there was not much space left for such existential issues. So a search for a new ethical and anthropological orientation started.

"Philosophy of man" was raised once again as a fundamental ideological theme. The Marxists tried to develop it within the context of their own authentic tradition. This meant a rediscovery of the inspiring and pioneering thought of the young Karl Marx, especially of his 1844 *Philosophical and Economic Manuscripts.* The concept of alienation emerged in the center of these new discussions. Is this concept valid also in a socialist society? And if it is, as many had clearly to recognize, how was one to interpret it and cope with it?

In this connection, the heritage of the non-Marxist tradition proved to be rather relevant. The existentialist philosophy which for years was considered as a typical decadent product of bourgeois society was taken more seriously again. The same applied to modern poetry and literature, especially to those streams struggling with the problem of evil, with ambiguities of the situation of man in the twentieth century, with its new threats. Franz Kafka, the important Prague thinker and writer of the twenties, was rediscovered again, and with him all his problems: the place of man within the alienating structures of institutional manipulations as they evidently appeared also within the centralized structure of socialist society. The theme of modern art and literature was clearly recognized as urgent and relevant for our own social and spiritual situation.

Did this new intellectual ferment also imply a new

approach to the Christian tradition? Not immediately and not in a direct way; with some delay and hesitations. This can be well understood; for a Marxist a theological answer is a mystical and, therefore, illegitimate answer to human problems. Yet some of the classical themes of Christian theology reappeared on the horizon of these new Marxist thinkers—not as answers but as questions: the problem of personal identity, the question of guilt and sin, the phenomenon of prayer, and many others. They were no longer dismissed as basically irrelevant, nonsensical. They were acknowledged as legitimate. This was, of course, an important change; a new possibility of encounter and exchange between Christians and Marxists was gradually opened.

If I should indicate the most important change in this respect, I would characterize it as a rediscovery of the significance of *biblical tradition*. This tradition had been rather eclipsed in the first years of socialist society. The cultural revolution sometimes· was conceived of as an up-rooting or at least as a silencing of the Christian heritage. This led to rather dismal cultural and even ideological consequences. Cultural: from the three basic sources of modern European culture (biblical, Greek, modern science), the first was nearly eliminated from public education and public cultural life. Ideological: by eclipsing this part of European tradition the Marxists themselves became cut off from one of the decisive streams of their genuine inspiration. They lost track of the biblical vision of dynamic history as a meaningful, unfinished, and open process and its prophetic passion for social justice, which were so important for Karl Marx himself. Thus, much of their original creativity was lost, and the static and dogmatic "established" elements prevailed—to the considerable detriment of creative Marxian thought itself.

This has fundamentally changed in the last years. The Marxists discovered the originality of biblical thinking and its unique significance for their own thought—in many respects greater than Greek metaphysics or nineteenth-century science. Thus the biblical stream of European tradition was recognized again as valid and important, both culturally and ideologically. As one of the leading Marxist thinkers put it in the title of his inspiring contribution published in a series of articles in the leading literary journal in Prague in 1967: "God Is Not Quite Dead" (V. Gardavský). The biblical heritage is deeply meaningful. And this means that Christians and Marxists may again become partners in an authentic dialogue.

A MUTUAL INTERPELLATION   "The caravan set out on the march." What was the progress of its march? What is the *meaning of dialogue?*

Many possible answers could be given to these questions. If I should choose one of the most important and already effective features, I would suggest "mutual interpellation." This catchword was coined by a French Marxist (who became important also in the Czechoslovak situation), Roger Garaudy, in his effort to characterize a hopeful and meaningful form of dialogue. Certain forms of "dialogue" lead to a deadlock. There is a "dialogue of the deaf" (those who persist in old concepts and are incapable of hearing new voices). And there is a "dialogue of beautiful souls" (those who indulge in mutual idealizations and cheap accommodation). Neither the one nor the other possibility is really fruitful. Only a critical and dialectic confrontation in seeking truth and common responsibility is of value. In such a confrontation, the interpellation of the partner, his own specific "alien" emphasis, may help to check the notorious (and therefore very often forgotten) temptations and shortcomings of one's own tradition.

The trend of such an interpellation could be formulated as follows: The special contribution of the Marxists is to remind Christians of the importance of historical and social "immanence." The special charisma of Christians is to bear witness to the Marxists about the relevance of "transcendence." This formulation may be somewhat simplified, but considering the basic streams of their respective traditions it may be justified. Now, does this mutual interpellation really work?

It is my deep conviction that it does indeed work. My conviction is validated by concrete experiences from the Christian-Marxist dialogue and from its repercussions for many representative thinkers on both sides. This became especially clear to me at one concrete occasion, the symposium organized jointly by (predominantly Roman Catholic) Paulus Gesellschaft and by the Czechoslovak Academy of Sciences in Mariánské Lázně, Marienbad, in 1967. The dialogue has developed many forms and even institutions. This great gathering of representative Marxist, Protestant, and Catholic thinkers, held for the first time in Eastern Europe, was in many respects one of the highlights of contemporary Christian-Marxist dialogue. Let me use this concrete example to demonstrate some aspects of mutual interpellation.

We start with the *Christian* side. Let us recall: the interpellation which Marxists address to Christians concerns their neglect of immanence. What was the situation at Mariánské Lázně?

One who was accustomed to the concept of Christianity as some kind of metaphysics or private matter was bound to be intrigued by the contributions theologians presented at Mariánské Lázně. From the very beginning a very different tone could be heard in the Christian expositions.

First, a strong emphasis on the historical and social dimensions of human life was presented. This was very clear in the contribution of a young German Roman priest, Johannes Metz. His lecture was a passionate criticism of the traditional retreat of Christianity into the private sphere characteristic of theology since the period of the Enlightenment. This theology operated when explaining the Bible message, primarily with the categories of intimacy and privacy. The social dimensions of faith were secondary and subordinate. The life of faith then took place primarily in the sphere of personal I-Thou relations. At present, it is necessary to revise this attitude, emphasized Professor Metz. To ignore the social context means that the very aspect which this theology wants to emphasize is missed: personal existence. No existence in this modern world is not deeply involved in the social and historical structures of this world. The Bible points in the same direction. The central message of the Bible refuses to be relegated to the private sphere. The content of the eschatological promises—freedom, peace, justice, reconciliation—call ever again to social responsibility. The church which wants to do justice to its calling must aim at becoming "an institution of creative social criticism" —otherwise it becomes, in this modern world, the salt which had lost its salinity.

This emphasis on the social responsibility of the church includes, second, an open approach to social revolution. According to Metz, "If Christian love is mobilized as the unconditional will to freedom, then this love may also command revolutionary violence." Another well-known Roman Catholic Italian theologian, Giulio Girardi, put forward several theses concerning revolution, emphasizing the significance of nonviolent revolutionary actions. In all instances the traditional, simply conservative, attitude of the church was questioned from theological positions—

among others, by the eminent French theologian Yves Congar.

Third, the same applied to the traditional triumphalism and ecclesiocentrism of the church. The hope which we proclaim is not the hope of a church-centered religion but the hope of the kingdom of God as the future of the world. The church cannot claim for itself privileges which it would deny to others. For instance, freedom understood merely as religious freedom and not as the freedom of man in the full sense of the word is incomplete freedom. "Privileges are the perversion of freedom."

This last quotation is taken from the lecture by Protestant theologian Jürgen Moltmann. It indicates that the new emphasis is shared by both Catholic and Protestant theologians. In this sense at Mariánské Lázně, in spite of all confessional fronts, some kind of consensus among the most distinctive theologians emerged. They were united in all these respects: first, in appreciation of the significance of historical and social dimensions; second, in their dynamic approach to social reality; and third, in a universalistic view of history. This means that if more than one of the aspects here emphasized belongs to the classical tenets of the Marxist revolutionary tradition, then it is evident that the interpellation of the Marxists among the Christians did not fall on barren soil.

Let us now turn our attention to the situation in the *Marxist* camp. What is the result of mutual interpellation for Marxists? Let us recall that such an interpellation should lead to a greater attention to the motive of transcendence and consequently to a differentiated approach to the problem of the church and religion. Indeed, this tendency was apparent in a number of Marxist contributions.

This is valid especially with respect to the problem of

transcendence, which was presented very strongly in the contributions by Czech Marxists. In his lecture before the symposium, Milan Prucha made a remarkable attempt to develop a new Marxist approach to the problem of man. He did so on the background of the classical philosophical approach to the problem of being. Prucha clearly refused to reduce the anthropological problem to the historical and social dimensions of man. It is true that man is a historical and a social being, but these important dimensions of human life do not represent the full range of humanity. In this connection, the question of real transcendence was posed. Prucha answered it by a reference to the concept of being, which must not be fixed prematurely either through the concept of matter (as in the case of traditional materialism) or through the concept of God (as is the case in religious tradition). In this connection Prucha undertook a criticism of theology from an unexpected angle. He confessed that, in the course of the Marxist-Christian dialogue, "our Christian friends have awakened in us the courage and appetite for transcendence." But the question must be referred back to them and radicalized. Christians do not manage to keep the problem of transcendence in its true profoundness but tend to link transcendence with "particularity." This is evident from the fact that they immediately "define" transcendence by the concept "God."

A philosopher must avoid this step. Face to face with this theological temptation, Marxism has a chance for interpellation of a different type than in the past. In the future, it might be its task not so to apply the brake on the Christian hankering after transcendence but, on the contrary, to free it from its religious trammels.

If the Christian-Marxist symposium brought a remarkable new accent to the Marxist approach to the problem of transcendence, it brought no less important contributions to the Marxist *theory of religion*. Attention was attracted particularly by the exposé of Robert Kalivoda. Kalivoda repudiated the misunderstanding that Marx's sentence about religion as "the opium of the people" could serve as the exclusive basis of a Marxist theory of Christianity. "The Alpha and Omega of Marxism is the discovery of dialectics of actual reality." If for more than one thousand years Christianity had almost the exclusive ideological monopoly in European history, it is evident that it could not be a sheer opium. The reality of European history was dialectical, not linear. Thus Christianity also played a dialectical role. No doubt it served also as "opium," as the ideology of conservative social and political power. But in its original and authentic form it was also a revolt against the injustices of this world, and it played a progressive role particularly in strong trends of Christian nonconformism (for example that of the Hussites). For this reason a Marxist theoretician of religion must differentiate in his approach to Christianity.

The voices of Garaudy, Machovec, Prucha, Kalivoda, and Kadlecová (and of a number of other creative Marxists at Mariánské Lázně and on other occasions) spoke convincingly of the fact that the interpellation of the Christians (their theological work of the last decades and especially their changed practice of the last few years) did not fall into empty space among the Marxists. It has become, in some of its aspects, an impetus to a new creative unfolding of Marxist theory and practice.

ECCENTRICITY OF DIALOGUE   The process and progress of Christian-Marxist dialogue initiated important shifts of emphasis and discoveries within both traditions. How should these changes be assessed? As an outbreak of a general ideological confusion in which all of the distinctive positions are blurred and where it no longer can be distinguished who is who? Is the eventual outcome of the dialogue an amorphous mixture of something like a semi-Marxist Christianity or semi-Christian Marxism?

Such an interpretation would utterly miss the mark. The very meaning of a mutual interpellation points in the opposite direction: dialogue does not mean indifference but, on the contrary, an encounter in difference: an interpellation. It was typical that at Mariánské Lázně both patriarchs of European dialogue, J. L. Hromádka and Roger Garaudy, very strongly emphasized the clear distinctions between the two positions. To listen carefully to the partner's interpellation does not mean to betray one's own tradition. When a theologian rediscovers the relevance of the social dimension he does not substitute *Das Kapital* for his Bible. And when the Marxist tries to take the problem of transcendence more seriously he does not convert to religious transcendentalism. Under the pressure of mutual confrontation a creative process of rethinking and rediscovery of one's own creative possibilities may develop. The authentic dialogical genius of both traditions is refreshed and revived from dogmatic slumber. And this is, without any doubt, a hopeful and promising possibility—for Marxists and Christians.

Many of us who participated in the Christian-Marxist dialogue are grateful for the experience of such a possibility. Yet this positive possibility would be misused and perverted if it were conceived as a final aim in itself. This is a real danger. The encouraging experience of a new understanding and the joy of a new mutual trust could easily degenerate into a clan spirit of something like a veterans' club. The pageantry of such a club may be colorful—but for the rest of the world it is utterly irrelevant. This need not necessarily be a tragedy for a veterans' club, but it would be an agonizing condition for both Christians and Marxists. For a self-centered Christianity plus a self-centered Marxism equals a blank betrayal of their authentic heritage and vision.

Let us recall what we emphasized at the beginning of our analysis: Christianity and Marxism are not only dialogical but also *eccentric* ways of thought and life. This means that the very impulse which has led to their new encounter necessarily leads them beyond themselves. They cannot remain just "each other's theme." Their mutual interpellation opens transcending horizons of their common historical, social, and spiritual responsibility. Here lies our new and common frontier, in concrete national societies (as we shall presently indicate in the example of Czechoslovakia in 1968) and internationally facing the basic problems of our contemporary world—concretely, the issues of technological and social revolutions.

In our world today all of us are confronted with unparalleled potentialities of both destruction and construction. More than ever the very survival of mankind depends on the unceasing implementation of social and historical responsibility. Not all movements of our times are aware of this situation; not all the philosophical and spiritual traditions, and certainly not the amorphous public opinion in our affluent and consuming societies. The moods of private disengagement, of consumer mentality, and worst of all, of fatalism seem to prevail.

Exactly here lies the most important frontier of Christian-Marxist dialogue. We shall be sober about its outreach and effect. Possibly both Christianity and Marxism are really two minority sects in a sea of indifference. Yet, they are two "sects" of people who are urged by the deepest motives of their convictions to challenge the fatalism and indifference and to be concerned about historical and social responsibility. They differ in the motives of their engagement and in the final vision of their hope. They raise their different and distinctive voices. Yet they live, if they live authentically, in that perspective of engagement and hope. If their mutual interpellation makes them a little more awake for these implications of their own spirit, it cannot be quite meaningless—even for those outside both camps. Christian-Marxist dialogue might become a modest yet important instrument in the imminent all-human struggle for a greater justice, for a more human world of man—today and tomorrow.

COOPERATION FOR THE HUMANIZATION OF SO-CIETY The eccentricity of the dialogue was illustrated in a very vivid and effective way in Czechoslovakia in 1968. Christians and Marxists, partners in a developing dialogue, became with new urgency the partners of political and social cooperation. The context of this new task was the classical and radical political problem: the task of *humanization* of our society. This was only logical. The anthropological issues were in the center of the theoretical dialogue; the cooperation for an effective humanization of our society was necessarily the core of our practical coexistence. What was the basic frontier of that endeavor?

If I should suggest a tentative outline of the common program of humanization I could—as a Christian— hardly find a better formulation than the following statement by Kari Marx: "To overthrow all conditions under which man is an oppressed, enslaved, destitute, and despised being." This is certainly no definition of humanization. There is no easy definition of this concept. Humanization is, among Marxists and Christians, a controversial and ambiguous concept. It is naturally closely connected with their respective concepts of man. Christians and Marxists differ in their ultimate answers to the anthropological problem. And yet as a penultimate consensus term, as a "middle axiom" of humanization, this concept proved to be meaningful for our cooperation and dialogue. It geared our common search and common action by setting an illuminating and inspiring standard for our decisions. In the light of this program, what was the situation in our society?

1. If we use such a standard to measure the revolutionary changes and the development of our socialist society, we have to acknowledge that some of the most dehumanizing conditions have been effectively changed. Some of the grave social problems have been basically solved, and some of the basic needs of men have been met. Let me list some of them.

We have no problem of poverty. There is no bitter poverty in the absolute sense; no one is really hungry or undernourished. And we have no acute problem of relative poverty, such as exists within some of the world's richest countries, for example, the United States. In other words, there are no grave contrasts between the "relative rich" and the "relative poor." The differences in the economic status of different groups and individuals of our society are very small. In this sense we are an emerging classless society. This has important moral connotations. The status of the traditional lower classes, for example, the working class, has grown considerably, which is an important moral and psychological manifestation of humanization.

We can point to other gains also: the national health service and its far-reaching and generous medical care, which is unconditionally at the disposal of all citizens; the educational system, open to all and free of any charge on all its levels. All these phenomena are connected with the basic structural change of our society, with the socialization of our economy. This revolutionary process has always had its problems and dangers. Fundamentally, however, I dare to consider the revolution and evolution of our society as an important step forward in the process of the humanization of society.

2. This assessment of socialism as a positive possibility of humanization in a developed society does not claim that the establishment of a socialist order means the solution of our problems. It does not mean the Kingdom of God will be realized. The problem of humanization is not solved in all its aspects. On the contrary, it poses some new and rather serious questions.

If we apply again our "middle axiom," we must concede that not all the conditions under which man is "an oppressed, enslaved, destitute, and despised being" have been utterly overthrown. As a matter of fact, some new serious features of dehumanization have emerged in the process of the socialist revolution and evolution.

If I were to point to the most important one, I would describe it as a certain tendency toward a monopoly of power and a monopoly of truth. I do not intend to pass quick moral and theological judgments on these tendencies. This would be too simple. In a sense this inclination was historically understandable. A revolutionary change of such a depth, the breaking of the economic and social power of the ancient regime, was hardly possible without a radical overthrow of structures of the preceding social order.

The Marxist idea of the "dictatorship of the proletariat" cannot be questioned *a priori* if we accept socialism as a step forward on the path of humanization. In all probability it is a necessity of the postrevolutionary order in its first stage. The danger of such a postrevolutionary order is that it does not discern quickly enough the signs of the time. It is tempted to "eternalize" its monopoly and to prolong it beyond the point of possible justification, that is, beyond the stage of a firmly established socialist system.

This is, of course, an extremely difficult problem. Christian anthropology, with its deep insight into the structure of human selfishness and love for power, should make us very sober and unbiased in facing this problem. No wonder many socialist countries, including my own, have found it extremely difficult to resist this trend.

Rigid Stalinism became its incarnation. With some justification we speak of the "cult of personality," the monopoly of power in the hands of one omnipotent man and the monopoly of truth in one omniscient personality. Under such circumstances not all the conditions under which man is an oppressed being had been overthrown. The case for humanization of the social and political process remained a burning issue.

3. The name for humanization in such a socialist society is *democratization*. What do we understand by democratization? We mean an attitude of a mature socialist society which takes itself and its creed seriously. This means, of course, that it understands itself as moving toward a classless society, a society of citizens who are not antagonistic enemies of one another and of their own society but who are united in their common social interest. This common social interest does not exclude diversities of outlook, of opinion, of interest, and of creed. These differences are very real, and they create a manifold tension within the society. But it is a creative tension.

It does not weaken but rather enriches its community. Therefore, these differences have to be tolerated.

The citizen ceases to be the potential enemy of such a state. Every citizen should, therefore, get his own fair share. This is valid in all respects: politically, culturally, ideologically. The monopoly of power and the monopoly of truth are overcome. In an open, democratic socialist society a deeper unity of citizens is achieved: unity in equality and freedom. To put it in a famous statement of Rosa Luxemburg: "No democracy without socialism, but also no socialism without democracy!" Thus a model of society emerges which might be considered as a substantial step forward on the way of humanization. It is a model of society which, on the one hand, has broken the basic bondage of economic inequality and oppressive financial power and, on the other hand, is applying democratic brakes to the monopoly of political power and truth.

This aim could correspond to the deepest humanistic insights both of the Marxists and of the Christians. From the Marxist point of view, the fundamental appeal of Karl Marx "to overthrow all conditions under which man is an oppressed, enslaved, destitute, and despised being" would come nearer to its fulfillment. And from the Christian point of view, democratic socialism could correspond to some degree to basic insights of the biblical faith of the Old and New Testaments. I mean again the prophetic vision of social justice oriented toward those who are underprivileged, the checking of the presumptions and arrogance of the privileged ones, and the apostolic message upholding the unalienable freedom and right of every individual man who is not a slave but a son in Jesus Christ.

Here is a worthy theme and goal for dialogue and

cooperation between Christians and Marxists—and all citizens of good will within a socialist society.

The events of August, 1968, shattered this endeavor. The way for a democratic socialism became narrower and more difficult. The fervor of a majority of Czechoslovak citizens was tamped down. No doubt also some of our own illusions were disclosed and uprooted. Dazzled by the inspiring vision of a new type of socialism and by the general support of our population which this model evidently received, we underestimated the international context of our effort. We had to pay for this bitterly. Yet the goal and the way of a democratic socialism was by no means discredited. The experience of human values opened in the process of renewal in our society was too genuine and deep to be forgotten or given up. It remains a model of hope and of the future—for many of our Marxists and for our Christians in a Marxist society.

70 71 72 73 10 9 8 7 6 5 4 3 2 1